Multimedia Technologies for Training

Multimedia Technologies for Training
An Introduction

Ann E. Barron
University of South Florida

Gary W. Orwig
University of Central Florida

Illustrated by Ted Newman

Cover Art by Ted Newman
and Nick Lilavois

1995
LIBRARIES UNLIMITED, INC.
Englewood, Colorado

Sponsored in part by Analysis and Technology, Inc.

LIBRARIES UNLIMITED, INC.
P.O. Box 6633
Englewood, CO 80155-6633
1-800-237-6124

Project Editor: Kevin W. Perizzolo
Copyeditor: Tama J. Serfoss
Proofreader: Eileen Bartlett
Indexer: Christine J. Smith
Interior Design and Type Selection: Alan Livingston

Original manuscript prepared with Microsoft Word 5.0 for Macintosh. Manuscript edited and prepared for production using Microsoft Word for Windows 2.0c. The book was typeset using Corel Ventura 4.2 with the following fonts:

Chapter Numbers: LiquidCrystal 40/30
Heads: Architecture 16/17.64, 14/15.41, 13/14.33
Scenario Heads: Technical 14/15.44
Scenario Text: Technical 11/12
Glossary/Index Heads: LiquidCrystal 30/22.5
Body Text: Palm Springs 10/11

The artwork was created in Autodesk 3-D Studio 3.0 and CorelDRAW! 4.0. Artwork was exported through CorelDRAW! as encapsulated postscript files for use in Corel Ventura.

Final camera ready pages were printed on a Unity LaserMaster 1200XL-T Plain Paper Typesetter.

Library of Congress Cataloging-in-Publication Data

Barron, Ann E.
   Multimedia technologies for training : an introduction / Ann E. Barron, Gary W. Orwig.
     xv, 211 p. 17x25 cm.
   Includes bibliographical references and index.
   ISBN 1-56308-262-4
   1. Educational technology. 2. Multimedia systems. 3. Teaching--Aids and devices. I. Orwig, Gary W., 1945- . II. Title.
LB1028.3.B36   1994
371.3'078--dc20   94-36876
                                                                CIP

Contents

INTRODUCTION

Video-CD, HDTV, Virtual Reality, and Wireless LANs . . . trainers in business, industry, and higher education are constantly bombarded with new technologies and terminology. New technologies emerge so quickly and relentlessly that it is almost impossible to keep up with the developments.

Multimedia Technologies for Training: An Introduction is designed for all trainers interested in bridging the technology gap. By "trainers" we are referring to anyone who is, or who intends to be, a manager, teacher, or instructional designer in an industrial, military, or academic training department. The book is intended for those currently employed in these professions as well as those planning a career in adult education.

The purpose of this book is to promote the use of new technologies and improve the instructional process in lifelong learning. Chapter 1 presents the issues and benefits of multimedia technology. The remaining chapters provide overviews of technologies, including compact discs, digital video, digital audio, authoring systems, virtual reality, networks, telecommunications, and teleconferencing. The training applications of each topic are examined in depth, and the advantages and disadvantages of each are outlined.

Organization and Use

Multimedia Technologies for Training: An Introduction can be used as a resource book or as a textbook. As a resource, this book provides a wealth of information. Each chapter begins with a "real-life" scenario depicting the use of technology in a training setting. A list of topics provides an outline of the chapter's contents. Detailed graphics throughout the book provide configurations and illustrations of hardware, software, and the like. In addition, each chapter contains contact information for software and hardware vendors. A detailed index and easy-to-understand glossary for the entire book provide easy access to specific topics and information.

As a textbook, *Multimedia Technologies for Training: An Introduction* is appropriate for technology courses at both the undergraduate and graduate levels. Throughout the book, emphasis is placed on the training applications of the various technologies. In addition, the advantages and disadvantages of each technology are discussed. To facilitate workshops and seminars, each chapter was written to be used independent of the others, although pertinent topics are cross-referenced.

ACKNOWLEDGMENTS

We would like to extend our appreciation to the management of Analysis & Technology, Inc. (A&T) for sponsoring this book. A&T has been producing quality multimedia programs for military and industrial customers for more than 10 years. The input of the trainers, instructional designers, programmers, graphic artists, and editors was invaluable to the production of this text, and the availability of the resources at A&T provided the opportunities necessary for the authors to use and examine the technologies. In particular, we would like to thank Gary Bennett, Joe Marino, and Susan Varnadoe for their support and encouragement.

Ann E. Barron
Gary W. Orwig

Training With Multimedia Technologies

A Scenario

Imagine that you are an engineer at a large electric power plant. Your responsibilities include overseeing the maintenance of the equipment in the power plant and training other employees in its use. It's Monday morning and you've just come back from a great weekend. As you walk through the plant toward your office, you hear the familiar sound of the steam turbine generator systems. It's a mild day, and only two of the units are running. Something sounds a little bit different today, but you aren't sure what it is.

After you have settled in for the morning, listened to your voice mail messages, and attended to the accumulated electronic mail on your computer, you lean back in your chair and listen to the faint sounds that carry through the office walls. There still seems to be a subtle difference in the sound of the generators.

You reach for your mouse and click on a microphone icon on the computer screen. From the menu that appears, you select the live microphones that are located on the two turbines that are operating and record short sound samples from each generator. With simple mouse clicks, you play back these audio samples several times. Another mouse click displays the actual waveform of a sample that sounds suspicious. The waveform looks a bit different than normal, so you retrieve an audio sample that was collected a month ago after routine maintenance and compare the two waveforms. Yes, there is a noticeable difference.

The change is clearly in the low frequency range and is unlike any bearing or rotor problem you have seen before. With a couple more clicks of your mouse, you call up an expert system "troubleshooter" and transfer the waveform of the sound over to it. The expert system analyzes the waveform and responds that it has never "heard" a similar waveform, but it rules out a number of causes for the change. The system concludes that there is a 70 percent chance that the problem can be found in the shock mounting system of the steam turbine.

Another click of your mouse pulls up last month's maintenance record for that turbine; the notes and digital photographs indicate that the mounting bolts had been tested at that time. A note attached to one image indicates that three adjacent bolts found to be loose were tightened during the maintenance check.

You now make one of those decisions that can cost a lot of money if it is wrong—you order a full transfer over to a third generator. This transfer results in spinning the third unit up and bringing the questionable unit down. After the system has stabilized, you send a team of mechanics to evaluate the mounting bolts. They find that the same three bolts are completely loose and that the probable cause is an apparent defect in the mounting bracket. You send an X-ray team to examine the bracket, and they bring back a digital image that confirms a flaw in the bracket.

Because you have never encountered this problem before, you immediately set up a two-way videoconference with the bracket manufacturer to view the image and discuss the cause. After careful analysis, the manufacturer confirms that the problem is new and suggests that you examine the two spare brackets on hand before installing them. To help train the maintenance technicians, the manufacturer uploads a multimedia lesson with digitized video clips of the replacement process.

You download the training program to the local area network (LAN) and send an e-mail message to the repair team that they should review the procedure using the multimedia program before replacing the brackets. Next, you confirm to the expert system that the mount was indeed the problem and update the databases to reflect the events of the day. Meanwhile, the company computer programmers are working to connect the expert system trouble shooter directly to the microphones for continuous real-time analysis. You wonder if the expert system will eventually become better at catching this kind of problem than you are.

* * * *

Multimedia technologies are becoming prevalent in business, military, and educational environments. This chapter examines the benefits of using technology for training and includes suggestions for planning and development. Topics covered in the chapter include:

- Technology in training
- Benefits of multimedia technology in training
- Multimedia planning and development guidelines
- A list of professional organizations and journals for further information

Technology in Training

Technology is an integral part of most businesses. Point-of-sale computer systems in retail stores track all purchases, inventory, and sales; most office workers have personal computers on their desktops; factories are automated; and worldwide business teleconferences are common. Fax machines and electronic mail are changing the way businesses exchange information, and telephone and cable companies are competing with each other to develop interactive technologies. Few people doubt the power of technology when it comes to information processing and transmission, data analysis, and the automation of routine tasks.

According to experts, the market for interactive technology could reach $14 billion by 1995, and many people "believe that the development of interactive media is equal in importance to the development of railroads" (Solomon 1993, 44). As technology becomes more available, affordable, and standardized, companies and educational institutions are turning to interactive multimedia as a part of their training programs. A 1993 survey of the Fortune 1000 companies conducted by a research firm in Massachusetts, found that "45 percent of the larger companies are already using multimedia technologies to do a portion of their in-house training" (Fryer 1994, 56).

Multimedia training applications may be developed in many forms, including tutorials, simulations, virtual reality, expert systems, or "just in time" training embedded in performance support systems. Technology is also enhancing training with the transmission, delivery, and storage of interactive lessons through networks, telecommunications, and optical media.

Benefits of Multimedia Technology in Training

Multimedia can be loosely defined as computer-based technology integrating some, but not necessarily all, of the following: text, graphics, animation, sound, and video. Instructional multimedia refers to applications designed to target specific learning objectives. Instructional multimedia has been embraced in training environments because it combines the interactivity and management features of computer-based training with the benefits of realistic audio and video.

Numerous research studies on instructional multimedia have been published in the past 10 years. However, the field is extremely diverse and complex, and it is difficult to generalize the findings. One confounding factor is that many of the technologies are still emerging and have not been fully examined. This section contains summaries of analyses and case studies related to the effectiveness and benefits of instructional multimedia.

Increased Effectiveness. To date, most of the research on the effectiveness of technology in training has been conducted with media comparison studies (comparing a group trained using instructional multimedia with a group trained by traditional means). The "results of these studies usually show no differences in outcomes between the groups" (Kearsley 1993, 34).

The apparent lack of difference could suggest that the variables were too complex or were not properly controlled, the media comparison was an inappropriate design for the study, or the results were assessed over too short a time frame.

Two separate meta-analyses that did note significant differences between multimedia instruction and conventional instruction were conducted by Fletcher (1990) and McNeil and Nelson (1991). The Fletcher meta-analysis reviewed 47 studies that compared interactive videodisc lessons with conventional approaches. He found that interactive videodisc was more effective and that the improvement was "roughly equivalent to increasing the achievement of students at the 50th percentile to that of students currently at the 69th percentile" (1990, v). The McNeil and Nelson analysis compared 63 studies that investigated the cognitive achievement of interactive video instruction. Their results indicated that interactive video "is an effective form of instruction" (1991, 5). Multimedia instruction can also benefit performance-based skills. For example, Federal Express estimated a 30 percent decrease in performance errors as the result of an interactive videodisc training program (Fryer 1994).

Self-confidence. Whether or not there is a significant difference in the effectiveness of multimedia instruction over conventional means, there is substantial evidence that students completing technology-based programs have an improved sense of mastery of the materials (Indiana 1990, Nurss 1989). Positive student perceptions can impact student motivation and decrease student attrition (Rachal 1993).

Reduced Training Time. Studies of the time required to train employees with multimedia and computer-based instruction have consistently found a reduction of 30 percent or more over conventional training (Fletcher 1990, Janson 1992, Ljungstrom and Sorensen 1993). For example, a multimedia training program implemented by Holiday Inn has reduced training time from an estimated 14 days to 6 days (Fryer 1994).

In most businesses, time is money, and the cost of employee time spent attending training is high. Instructional methods that can reduce training time decrease training costs. "Even a small reduction in participant time could make a large impact; for instance, a five percent reduction in training time could save employee time worth $8 billion dollars a year" (Dennis 1994, 25).

Decreased Cost. Although the start-up costs for multimedia are high, multimedia training can be cost-effective over the long run. Fletcher (1990) found a favorable cost ratio for multimedia versus conventional training in military, industry, and academic environments. In other words, Fletcher found that multimedia training is less costly than traditional means. Decreased cost for multimedia training appears "to be linked to savings due to use of multimedia versus real equipment, multimedia versus costs of human delivery, or decentralized versus centralized instruction" (Oklahoma University 1993, 1–10). For example, United Airlines estimated a $9 million saving in travel, hotel, and other expenses when they implemented a $150,000 interactive training program (Fryer 1994).

Active Learning. Multimedia involves students in active, rather than passive, learning through physical interaction and cognitive engagement (Oblinger 1993). For example, students may be required to answer questions, make menu selections, or provide other meaningful inputs in a program.

Active learning can serve to maintain attention, create new knowledge, and improve achievement (Alessi and Trollip 1991, Hannafin 1993).

Multisensory Delivery. Research in learning styles indicates that some students learn better through specific modalities, such as visual, audio, or kinesthetic (Barbe and Swassing 1979, Dunn and Dunn 1978). Some students are visual learners, some learn through hearing, and some learn by touch. Multimedia provides instruction through multiple sensory channels, allowing students to use the sensory modes that they prefer (Oblinger 1993).

Multilingual Delivery. Multimedia instruction can include multiple audio tracks with several different languages. A major benefit of using multimedia training in companies with diverse populations is the ability to instantly change instructional languages (Fryer 1994).

Encourage Exploration. Another advantage of multimedia training programs is that they can be nonlinear and allow students to explore the content from multiple perspectives (Cognition and Technology Group 1990). Multimedia programs that employ this methodology can "help students develop rich mental models as the basis for future learning; create environments that permit sustained exploration by students and teachers; help students explore the domain from multiple perspectives; and develop integrated knowledge structures that help students transfer knowledge to more complex tasks" (Moore, Myers, and Burton 1994, 34).

Motivation. Technology can inspire students by making learning interactive and relevant. Research studies generally agree that students are positively motivated by the integration of technology (Smith 1987, Tolman and Allred 1991, Barron and Kysilka 1992). The fact that students enjoy working with technology and, therefore, stay on tasks for longer periods of time, could be a valuable, long-term benefit (Summers 1990-91).

Increased Safety. Many environments are too dangerous for training programs. In these cases, it is often possible to design a multimedia program that enables the students to interact with simulations of the environment without safety hazards. For example, the U.S. Navy implemented a multimedia program to safely train signal officers to land aircraft on carriers (Tynan 1993).

Multimedia Planning and Development Guidelines

The initial costs of multimedia training programs are generally high, and the development time may be lengthy (Golas 1994). Even though multimedia technology has many benefits for training, it is not appropriate for all situations—a detailed needs analysis and investigation of other options is essential. Before embarking on a multimedia project, consider these suggestions:

1. Join professional organizations. There are many professional organizations that focus on multimedia design and development. By joining these groups, you will have access to their publications, conferences, and the experience of experts in multimedia production. A list of professional organizations related to instructional multimedia is included at the end of this chapter.

2. Subscribe to professional and technical magazines and journals. There is a wealth of multimedia information in periodicals such as trade journals, technical magazines, and professional publications. Many of these publications are available at little or no cost to qualified professionals. The contact information for many of these periodicals is included in the list of resources at the end of this chapter.

3. Attend professional conferences. Many professional organizations sponsor technology conferences. By attending workshops and seminars at the conferences, you will see and hear about the latest developments in instructional multimedia, meet others who are in the process of implementing multimedia, and gain insights on techniques and resources. Technology periodicals usually feature information about upcoming conferences.

4. Visit training sites at other locations. The best way to get ideas on integrating technology into your program is to visit other sites. Most businesses are more than willing to share what they have learned.

5. Invest in personnel with expertise in multimedia development. There is a definite learning curve for technology. An inexperienced team will require substantially more time to complete a project. In most cases, you can avoid costly mistakes, and save money by hiring personnel (either directly or through a vendor) with experience in the management and development of multimedia programs.

6. Investigate commercial applications. It is costly and foolish to "reinvent the wheel" when creating a multimedia training program. Before producing an application from scratch, check to see if there are commercial products available that would meet your needs. The *Multimedia and Videodisc Compendium for Education and Training* and various CD-ROM catalogs are the best sources for commercial products (see "Recommended Reading" at the end of this chapter).

7. Don't get carried away with bells and whistles. Because you have a multimedia computer that can play sounds and videos, does not mean that you need to include them in every program. Determine your training goals and objectives first, then select the best media to convey the content.

8. Build a prototype of the system. The planning, design, and development stages of multimedia applications are similar to those of traditional computer-based training. However, gathering and processing the multimedia components may take more time and require more up-front decisions (Ricciuti 1993). Building a rapid prototype early in the development process can help alleviate misconceptions and provide the look and feel of the finished product, before costly development efforts.

9. Balance "high tech" with "high touch." Multimedia should not be viewed as a replacement for human trainers or teachers but as another tool for providing access to knowledge. Human beings are

essential components for providing high-touch in an increasingly high-tech world (Cornell and Bollet 1989).

Conclusion

Instructional multimedia presents opportunities and challenges for training programs. Used appropriately, it can provide an excellent avenue for student motivation, exploration, and instruction in a multisensory, diverse world. Technology, however, is only a tool. The challenge rests with educators, instructional designers, and trainers to effectively integrate multimedia technology throughout the curriculum.

References

Barbe, W. B., and R. H. Swassing. 1979. *Teaching through modality strengths: Concepts and practices*. Columbus, OH: Zaner-Bloser.

Barron, A. E., and M. Kysilka. 1992. Research on the effectiveness of digital audio in computer-based education. Paper presented at the American Educational Research Association, April 20-24, San Francisco, CA.

Cognition and Technology Group at Vanderbilt. 1990. Anchored instruction and its relationship to situated cognition. *Educational Researcher* 19(5): 2-10.

Cornell, R. A., and R. M. Bollet. 1989. High touch in the high tech world of education: Impact '89. *Educational Media International* 26(2): 67-72.

Dennis, V. 1994. How interactive instructional saves time. *Journal of Instruction Delivery Systems* 8(1): 25-28.

Dunn, R., and K. Dunn. 1978. *Teaching students through their individual learning styles: A practical approach*. Reston, VA: Reston.

Fletcher, J. D. 1990. The effectiveness of interactive videodisc instruction in defense training and education. Arlington, VA: Institute for Defense Analyses, Science and Technology Division (IDA paper P-2372).

Fryer, B. 1994. Multimedia training. *Multimedia World* 1(7): 55-59.

Golas, K. C. 1994. Estimating time to develop interactive courseware in the 1990s. *Journal of Interactive Instruction Development*: 6(3): 3-11.

Indiana Opportunities Industrialization Center of America State Council. 1990. A comparative study of adult education Indianapolis/Richmond. Third party evaluator final report. Indianapolis: Author. (ERIC Document Reproduction Service No. ED327697).

Janson, J. L. 1992. Simulation program helps Coast Guard sink training costs. *PC Week Special Reports: Graphics* (January): 91-93.

Kearsley, G. 1993. Educational technology: Does it work? *ED-TECH Review* (Spring/Summer): 34-36.

Ljungstrom, L., and L. Sorensen. 1993. Interactive video in the training of engine drivers at the Danish state railways. *Multimedia and Videodisc Monitor* 11(2): 25-28.

McNeil, B. J., and K. R. Nelson. 1991. Meta-analysis of interactive video instruction: A 10 year review of achievement effects. *Journal of Computer-Based Instruction* 18(1): 1-6.

Moore, M. M., R. J. Myers, and J. K. Burton. 1994. Theories of multimedia and learning: What multimedia might do . . . and what we know about what it does. In *Multimedia and Learning*, ed. A. Ward. Alexandria, VA: National School Boards Association.

Nurss, J. R. 1989. PALS evaluation project. Atlanta: Georgia State University, Center for the Study of Adult Literacy. (ERIC Document Reproduction Service No. ED313573).

Oblinger, D. 1993. *Multimedia in instruction*. Chapel Hill, NC: The Institute for Academic Technology.

Rachal, J. R. 1993. Computer-assisted instruction in adult basic and secondary education: A review of the experimental literature, 1984-1992. *Adult Education Quarterly* 43(3): 165-72.

Ricciuti, M. 1993. Making multimedia work. *Datamation* 39 (September): 30.

Smith, E. E. 1987. Interactive video: An examination of use and effectiveness. *Journal of Instructional Development*, 10: 2-10.

Solomon, J. 1993. A risky revolution: business is scrambling to market interactive media, but pitfalls remain. *Newsweek* 121 (April): 44.

Summers, J. A. 1990-91. Effect of interactivity upon student achievement, completion intervals, and affective perceptions. *Journal of Educational Technology Systems* 19(1): 53-57.

Tynan, D. 1993. Multimedia goes on the job just in time. *NewMedia*, 3(7): 39-46.

University of Oklahoma. 1993. *Instructional technology effectiveness study*. Atlanta, GA: Skill Dynamics.

Professional Organizations

Association for Educational Communications and Technology (AECT), 1025 Vermont Avenue, N.W., Suite 820, Washington, DC 20005, 202-347-7839

Association for Information and Image Management (AIIM), 1100 Wayne Avenue, Suite 1100, Silver Spring, MD 20910, 301-587-8202

Association for the Development of Computer-Based Instructional Systems (ADCIS), 1601 W. Five Avenue, Suite 111, Columbus, OH 43212, 614-487-1528

Association of the Advancement of Computing in Education (AACE), P.O. Box 2966, Charlottesville, VA 22902, 804-973-3987

Association of Visual Communicators (AVC), 818-787-6800

EDUCOM, 1112 16th Street, N.W., Suite 600, Washington, DC 20036, 202-872-4200

Information Industry Association (IIA), 555 New Jersey Avenue, N.W., Suite 800, Washington, DC 20001, 202-639-8262

Interactive Multimedia Association (IMA), 3 Church Circle, Suite 800, Annapolis, MD 21401, 410-280-9293

International Communications Industries Association (ICIA), 3150 Spring Street, Fairfax, VA 22031-2399, 703-273-7200

International Interactive Communications Society (IICS), P.O. Box 1862, Lake Oswego, OR 97035, 503-649-2065

International Society for Technology in Education (ISTE), 1787 Agate Street, Eugene, OR 97403-1923, 503-346-4414

International Technology Education Association (ITEA), 1914 Association Drive, Reston, VA 22091-1502, 703-860-2100

Multimedia PC Marketing Council (MPC), 1730 M Street N.W., Suite 700, Washington, DC 20036-4510, 202-331-0494

Office of Technology Assessment (OTA), U.S. Congress, Washington, DC 20510-8025, 202-224-8996

Optical Publishing Association (OPA), P.O. Box 21268, Columbus, OH 43221, 614-793-9660

Society for Applied Learning Technology (SALT), 50 Culpeper Street, Warrenton, VA 22186, 800-457-6812

Software Publishers Association (SPA), 1730 M Street N.W., Washington, DC 20036, 202-452-1600

Multimedia-Related Journals and Magazines

Advanced Imaging, 445 Broad Hollow Road, Melville, NY 11747, 516-845-2700

Beyond Computing, 590 Madison Avenue, New York, NY 10022, 708-564-1385

CD-ROM Professional, 462 Danbury Road, Wilton, CT 06897, 800-248-8466

CD-ROM Today, 23-00 Route 208, Fair Lawn, NJ 07410, 201-703-9505

CD-ROM World, 11 Ferry Lane West, Westport, CT 06880, 800-635-5537

Collegiate Microcomputer, 5500 Wabash Avenue, Terre Haute, IN 47803, 812-877-1511

Communications of the ACM, P.O. Box 12114, Church Street Station, New York, NY 10257

Computer, 445 Hoes Lane, P.O. Box 13331, Piscataway, NJ 08855

Computers & Education, Fairview Park, Elmsford, NY 10523, 914-592-7700

Computers in Education, 1300 Don Mills Road, North York, Ontario M3B 3M8, 416-445-5600

Connect, Pegasus Press, Inc., 3487 Braeburn Circle, Ann Arbor, MI 48108, 800-GET-CONNECT

ED-TECH Review, P.O. Box 1966, Charlottesville, VA 22902, 804-973-3987

Education Computer News, 951 Pershing Drive, Silver Spring, MD 20910, 301-587-6300

Educational and Training Technology International, 120 Pentonville Road, London N1 9 JN UK, 44-0752-232374

Educational Information Resource, 1787 Agate Street, Eugene, OR 97403, 800-336-5191

Educational Technology News, 951 Pershing Drive, Silver Spring, MD 20910, 800-BPI-0122

Educational Technology Research and Development (ETR&D), 1126 16th Street N.W., Washington, DC 20036, 202-466-4780

Educational Technology, 720 Palisade Avenue, Englewood Cliffs, NJ 07632, 201-871-4007

Hypernexus: Journal of Hypermedia and Multimedia Studies, 1787 Agate Street, Eugene, OR 97403, 800-336-5191

Information Technology and Libraries, 50 East Huron Street, Chicago, IL 60611, 312-944-6780

Instruction Delivery Systems, 50 Culpeper Street, Warrenton, VA 22186, 703-347-0055

Internet World, Mecklermedia Corporation, 11 Ferry Lane W., Westport, CT 06880, 203-226-6967

Journal of Artificial Intelligence in Education, P.O. Box 2966, Charlottesville, VA 22902, 804-973-3987

Journal of Computer Information Systems, Oklahoma State University, Stillwater, OK 74078, 405-744-5090

Journal of Computer-Based Instruction, 1601 West Fifth Avenue, Suite 111, Columbus, OH 43212, 614-488-1863

Journal of Computing in Higher Education, Lederle Graduate Research Center, Amherst, MA 01003, 413-545-4232

Journal of Computing in Teacher Education, 1787 Agate Street, Eugene, OR 97403, 800-336-5191

Journal of Educational Computing Research, 26 Austin Avenue, Box 337, Amityville, NY 11701, 516-691-1270

Journal of Educational Multimedia and Hypermedia, P.O. Box 2966, Charlottesville, VA 22902, 804-973-3987

Journal of Educational Technology Systems, 26 Austin Avenue, Box 337, Amityville, NY 11701, 516-691-1270

Journal of Instruction Delivery Systems, 50 Culpeper St., Warrenton, VA 22186, 703-347-0055

Journal of Interactive Instruction Development, 50 Culpeper Street, Warrenton, VA 22186, 703-347-0055

Journal of Research on Computing in Education, 1787 Agate Street, Eugene, OR 97403, 800-336-5191

Journal of Technology and Teacher Education, P.O. Box 2966, Charlottesville, VA 22902, 804-973-3987

Library Hi Tech Journal, P.O. Box 1808, Ann Arbor, MI 48106, 313-434-5530

Mathematics and Computer Education, Box 158, Old Bethpage, NY 11804, 516-822-5475

Media & Methods, 1429 Walnut Street, Philadelphia, PA 10102, 215-563-3501

Microcomputers in Education, Two Sequan Road, Watch Hill, RI 02891, 203-655-3798

Multimedia & Videodisc Monitor, P.O. Box 26, Falls Church, VA 22040-0026, 703-241-1799

Multimedia Business Report, P.O. Box 7430, Wilton, CT 06897, 203-834-0033

Multimedia Review, 11 Ferry Lane West, Westport, CT 06880, 800-635-5537

Multimedia Schools, 462 Danbury Road, Wilton, CT 06897, 202-244-6710

Multimedia World, 501 Second Street, San Francisco, CA 94107, 415-281-8650

NewMedia, 901 Mariner's Island Boulevard, Suite 365, San Mateo, CA 94404, 415-573-5170

Online Access, 900 N. Franklin #310, Chicago, IL 60610, 312-573-1700

Optical Information Systems Magazine, 11 Ferry Lane West, Westport, CT 06880-5808, 203-226-6967

Presentation Products, P.O. Box 1174, Skokie, IL 60076-9715

Presentations Magazine, 50 S. Ninth Street, Minneapolis, MN 55402, 800-328-4329

Satellite Scholar, P.O. 3508, Missoula, MT 59806, 406-549-4860

T.H.E. Journal, 150 El Camino Real, Suite 112, Tustin, CA 92680, 714-730-4011

Tech Trends, 1126 16th Street N.W., Washington, DC 20036, 202-466-4780

Technology & Learning, 2451 East River Road, Dayton, OH 45439, 513-294-5785

Virtual Reality World, 11 Ferry Lane West, Westport, CT 06880, 602-887-4485

Wired, 544 Second Street, San Francisco, CA 94107, 415-904-0660

Recommended Reading

Ambrose, D. W. 1991. The effects of hypermedia on learning: A literature review. *Educational Technology* 31(12): 51-54.

Barron, A. E., and G. W. Orwig. 1993. *New technologies for education: A beginner's guide*. Englewood, CO: Libraries Unlimited.

Bosco, J. 1986. An analysis of evaluations of interactive video. *Educational Technology* 26(5): 7-17.

Bruder, I. 1991. Multimedia: How it changes the way we teach & learn. *Electronic Learning* 11(1): 22-26.

Brunner, C. 1990. What it really means to "integrate" technology. *Technology and Learning* 11(3): 12-14.

Bunnell, D. 1992. Let's start a revolution: Bring multimedia to education. *NewMedia* (January): 5.

Dalton, D. 1990. The effects of cooperative learning strategies on achievement and attitudes during interactive video. *Journal of Computer-Based Instruction* 17(1): 8-16.

DeBloois, M. 1988. Use and effectiveness of videodisc training. *The Videodisc Monitor* (June): 23-25.

Karraker, R. 1992. Crisis in American education: Can multimedia save the day? *NewMedia* (January): 523-27.

Kozma, R. B. 1991. Learning with media. *Review of Educational Research* 61(2): 179-211.

Maddux, D. D., D. L. Johnson, and J. W. Willis. 1992. *Educational computing: Learning with tomorrow's technologies*. Boston, MA: Allyn & Bacon.

Mareth, P. 1993. How multimedia will change our industries. *SMPTE Journal* (July): 605-6.

Miller, J. J. 1992. Multimedia. *PC Magazine* 11(6): 112-23.

Multimedia and Videodisc Compendium for Education and Training 1994. St. Paul, MN: Emerging Technology Consultants.

Nelson, T. 1993. Reaching into interactive waters. *NewMedia*, 3(11): 18.

Niemiec, R., and H. J. Walberg. 1987. Comparative effects of computer-assisted instruction: A synthesis of reviews. *Journal of Educational Computing Research* 3(1): 19-37.

Shaw, D. S. 1992. Computer-aided instruction for adult professionals: A research report. *Journal of Computer-Based Instruction* 19(2): 54-57.

Stefanae, S. 1994. Interactive advertising. *NewMedia*, 4(4): 43-52.

Steinberg, E. R. 1992. The potential of computer-based telecommunications for instruction. *Journal of Computer-Based Instruction* 19(2): 42-46.

Summers, J. A. 1990-91. Effect of interactivity upon student achievement, completion intervals, and affective perceptions. *Journal of Educational Technology Systems* 19(1): 53-57.

Tolman, M. H., and R. A. Allred. 1991. *The computer and education: What research says to the teacher.* (ERIC Document Reproduction Service No. ED335344).

Trotter, A. 1990. Multimedia instruction puts teachers in the director's chair. *Executive Educator* 12(7): 20-22.

Ward, A. W., ed. 1994. *Multimedia and Learning.* Alexandria, VA: National School Boards Association.

Wilson, K. 1991. New tools for new learning opportunities. *Technology & Learning* 11(7): 12-13.

CD-ROM and Compact Disc Technologies

2

A Scenario

Tyrone knew he had a problem; actually, he had several problems—sales were down, customer satisfaction was low, and his boss was upset. All of these issues seemed to stem from the fact that the sales personnel at the 125 branches of the auto parts stores could not locate parts for the customers in a timely fashion. In their defense, Tyrone realized that finding and recommending the correct part from the thousands available was not an easy task—there were nine large books to sort through, the indexes were cumbersome, and many of the parts were very similar.

After analyzing the possible alternatives, Tyrone decided to take a gamble and produce a CD-ROM for the sales force. First, he contacted the vendors who supplied the auto parts books and requested electronic versions of the data. Luckily, the vendors had them, and they could be tagged for search and retrieval by part number, part name, keywords, and location.

After Tyrone investigated the possible formats for the CD-ROM, he decided to create the disc in ISO 9660. He had learned that the ISO 9660 format could be accessed by either an MS-DOS or Macintosh computer. Next, he purchased the software to index and format the data. When Tyrone discovered that his textual information consisted of only 250 megabytes, he decided to add training clips to illustrate how to replace some of the more common auto parts. Diagrams (with five levels of zoom) of the parts were also linked to the information.

After the data were indexed and formatted, Tyrone created a preview or check disc by recording all of the formatted data on a CD-Recordable drive. The first attempt at recording the check disc failed because the source computer could not sustain a steady stream of data. Tyrone used a more powerful computer for the second attempt and was successful. Then he verified that the data were in the optimal structure, tested the access time, and corrected minor errors. Tyrone decided to have the rest of the discs recorded at a mastering studio because he needed 125 copies of the disc, and it would be less expensive.

The CD-ROM was not an instant success—many of the sales team resisted the change from their familiar patterns. Slowly, however, they began to realize the advantages of the compact disc, including the speed of information retrieval and its graphic and training capabilities. Now, as they reflect upon the past, they can't believe that at one time they actually thumbed through all those books to locate parts!

* * * *

Compact disc-read only memory (CD-ROM) technology is a key element in multimedia delivery. In industry, CD-ROM can provide fast access to information for sales and maintenance personnel, reduce the cost of sales, and improve customer service. In education, a rich variety of reference and multimedia applications are available to enhance the curricula. The topics of this chapter include:

- An overview of CD-ROM technology
- Commercial applications for CD-ROM
- Configurations for CD-ROM hardware
- Purchasing a CD-ROM drive
- Steps for Creating a CD-ROM disc
- Networking CD-ROMs
- Advantages and disadvantages of CD-ROM
- Compact disc standards and related technologies

Introduction

The first compact discs appeared on the market in 1982 and stored up to 74 minutes of high-quality music. The 4.72 inch compact discs were durable and programmable, but a major drawback was that they were "read only." When the technology emerged, many people predicted that it would fail because consumers could not record favorite songs or voices. Obviously, the predictions were wrong—audio CDs (also referred to as CD-Audio) are said to be "the most successful consumer electronics product in history" (Dataware Technologies 1993, 3).

In 1985, the same technology that was used to create audio CDs for music was applied to CD-ROM. Unlike CD-Audio, the digital information on a CD-ROM disc contains text, graphics, audio, and other media. When compared to the distribution costs of paper or diskettes, a compact disc provides an economical and durable way to publish and disseminate information.

Over 650 megabytes (MB) of data (roughly the equivalent of 460 high density computer diskettes or 250,000 pages of text) can be stored on a single

CD-ROM. This means a business with 20 volumes of technical manuals could use one CD-ROM for storage, allowing for flexibility, ease of storage, and quick access to a vast amount of information.

In order to provide rapid access to this huge quantity of information, most CD-ROM reference discs contain alphabetical indexes to help locate and retrieve the data quickly and accurately. To create an index, a software indexing program "tags" the words in the application and notes the location of each word (which articles or documents it appears in and the exact location within the text).

After the index is created, users can search for any word on the CD-ROM in a split second. The program searches for the word in the alphabetical index, retrieves the location information, and lists the number of times the word appears on the disc and the exact location of each appearance. If logical connectors (such as *and*, *or*, and *not*) are used for Boolean searches, the words in the indexes are cross-referenced.

It is important to note that CD-ROM discs are read-only; the information on the discs is permanent and cannot be modified or erased. The information is encoded on the disc by a laser, and the disc is also read optically. Because there is no direct, physical contact with the disc when it is played, CD-ROM discs have long life spans.

A major advantage of CD-ROM is the low cost of the storage medium. Figure 2.1 compares the relative costs of alternative storage and delivery of data. Each bar in the chart represents the approximate cost of storing one megabyte of information.

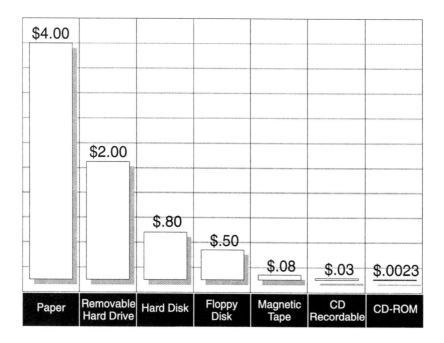

Fig. 2.1. Approximate cost per megabyte of storage based on current market prices.

Although CD-ROM technology did not achieve instant success when it was first introduced in 1985, there are currently thousands of CD-ROM titles available commercially. CD-ROM technology is now a standard in most computing markets, and many computer companies are building CD-ROM drives into their new computers. There is little doubt that CD-ROM technology will continue to play a central role in the development and distribution of multimedia applications in industry and education.

Commercial Applications

A CD-ROM disc can store information for a wide variety of applications. As the technology matures, CD-ROM developers are producing increasingly sophisticated programs with multimedia components. A growing number of companies are now offering cross-platform titles—applications that can run in either Microsoft Windows, MS-DOS, or Macintosh environments. Most CD-ROM applications fall within one of the following categories: encyclopedias, reference sources, databases, multimedia products, games, computer software, and clip media.

Encyclopedias

A useful and popular application of CD-ROM technology is the ability to store an entire encyclopedia on a single disc. In addition to the full-text of an encyclopedia, a CD-ROM can include a rich array of charts, graphics, pictures, video clips, and sound. The power of an electronic encyclopedia lies not only in the user's ability to rapidly find a particular article and its multimedia components, but also in the ability to locate information through multiple search paths such as timelines, keywords, pictures, or video. A real bonus is that the multimedia encyclopedias such as *Microsoft Encarta: Multimedia Encyclopedia*, the New Grolier *Multimedia Encyclopedia*, and Compton's *Multimedia Encyclopedia* are amazingly inexpensive.

Reference Sources

In addition to encyclopedias, other reference sources offer full-text information—dictionaries, government regulations, and maps are just a few of the examples. One useful reference tool is *Computer Select* by Ziff Communications, which provides up-to-date and full-text information from a multitude of computer magazines and specifications for thousands of hardware and software products. Another example is the *Street Atlas USA* by Delorme Publishing Company, which can display a street map of any location in the United States. Searches for areas can be specified by telephone number, zip code, or city.

Databases

CD-ROMs provide optimal storage for large databases such as *The National, Economic, Social, and Environmental DataBank* by the U.S. Department of Commerce. Allegro New Media used information from Standard and Poors to produce the *Business 500* disc, which provides a database of company descriptions, financial outlooks, and video clips of products. Another example of a CD-ROM database is the *ProPhone National Telephone Directory* by ProCD Inc., a six-disc set of searchable information that replaces 10,000 paper phone books. With CD-ROMs such as these, companies have fast, easy access to pertinent financial and economic information. The database vendors keep the information up-to-date by distributing revisions on a monthly or quarterly basis.

Multimedia

CD-ROMs can store digital information in any combination of text, graphics, sound, video, and animation, so they make an excellent medium for multimedia applications. Multimedia on a CD-ROM can range from interactive training programs with sound and video to electronic books with animated characters. For example, the *Mayo Family Health Book* by Interactive Ventures, Inc. provides interactive healthcare lessons that include video segments, animation sequences, illustrations, and sound.

Games

There are a wealth of games and entertainment discs now available on CD-ROM because of the sound and graphics enhancements possible. In *Sherlock Holmes, Consulting Detective,* by Icom Simulations, players can use Sherlock's address book, notebooks, and files to help solve mysteries. In addition, high-quality sound and video screens add realism as players "eavesdrop" as Holmes conducts interviews and interrogations.

Leading video game producers, such as Sega and Turbo Technologies, are now distributing games on compact discs. These games are played using special compact disc game players that attach to television sets. The games stored on compact discs provide more audio, animation, and graphic interactions than the former cartridge versions because of the larger storage space available.

Computer Software

Because a CD-ROM stores digital computer information, it is an ideal medium for distributing computer programs. Distribution via CD-ROM is advantageous because the information is read-only and the programs cannot be erased by accident. Another advantage is the price; it is much less costly to distribute large programs such as *CorelDRAW!* by Corel Corporation on one compact disc than on a dozen floppy diskettes. Many commercial software vendors provide customers with a collection of programs on CD-ROM.

The customer has the option to "unlock" a program by inputting a password code after payment is made. Shareware distributors such as PC-SIG also disseminate their products on CD-ROM.

Clip Media

Digital video and audio usually produce very large files that can be difficult to distribute on floppy diskettes. CD-ROM is an excellent medium for storage and distribution of these and other large image files. There are many commercial, royalty-free videoclips, images, and sounds available on CD-ROM that can be incorporated into sales presentations and computer-based training programs.

Hardware Configurations

To read and display the information on a CD-ROM disc, a CD-ROM player must be connected to a computer. CD-ROM players can be external or internal devices. The players usually have a headphone jack in the front of the player and speaker outputs in the back. If audio is recorded on the disc in CD-Audio format, it can be output directly from the CD-ROM player to headphones or speakers; if the audio is stored as digitized audio, it must be routed back through the computer (See chapter 4 for more information about digital audio).

Most external CD-ROM players can be connected to either a Macintosh or an MS-DOS computer with the proper interface cable. With the proper software, the computer can read the data on the CD-ROM as if it were a hard drive. In other words, you can do a directory listing or even copy files from the CD-ROM to a diskette or hard drive. A CD-ROM system (See fig. 2.2) requires the following components:

- Computer
- CD-ROM drive (player)
- CD-ROM disc
- Interface cable to connect the computer to the CD-ROM drive
- SCSI port or controller card in the computer
- Speakers or headphones (for audio)
- Software program to access the CD-ROM (CD-ROM drivers)

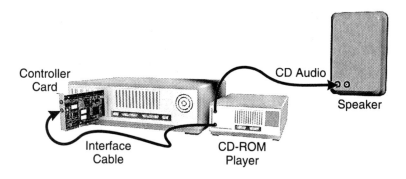

Fig. 2.2. Configuration for external CD-ROM.

Macintosh

A CD-ROM player can be connected to any Macintosh computer through the SCSI (Small Computer Serial Interface) port on the back of the computer. The required interface cable may be included with the purchase of the CD-ROM player or purchased separately. CD-ROM access files must be loaded into the Macintosh's system folder to enable the computer to communicate with the player. The access files alert the computer to the presence of the CD-ROM and provide the software protocols necessary to read the data on the CD-ROM. (The required software is generally included with the purchase of a CD-ROM drive.)

When purchasing a CD-ROM application for a Macintosh computer, be sure to verify that the computer can display the required number of colors. Most Macintosh CD-ROM applications will stipulate either monochrome, 16 colors, or 256 colors. Some of the CD-ROM programs are memory intensive and may require several megabytes of RAM and storage space on a hard drive.

MS-DOS

When purchasing a CD-ROM application for an MS-DOS computer, the application must be compatible with the computer, the monitor, and the audio sound card. If the CD-ROM program offers color graphics, video clips, and photographs, a VGA (video graphics array) monitor with at least 16 colors is required. If the program is text only, a monochrome or CGA (color graphics adapter) monitor may be sufficient. Programs with sound may require a specific audio card, or they may stipulate that the computer meet the MPC (Multimedia PC) standards (See chapter 4 for more information about MPC requirements).

When a CD-ROM player is connected to an MS-DOS computer, a proprietary controller card designed for the player can be installed, or a SCSI connection can be used. In either case, an interface cable connects the CD-ROM player to the port on the card or computer. In some cases, the CD-ROM can connect to the computer through an interface on the audio card (See chapter 4 for more information about audio cards).

When a CD-ROM player is installed, a software program (usually Microsoft *Extensions*) must be added on the start-up drive of the computer. These extensions allow the computer to communicate with the CD-ROM player as if it were another hard drive. In most cases, an install program will place all of the files in the appropriate locations.

Jukeboxes

A *jukebox* is a CD-ROM player that can automatically load one or more CD-ROMs. Between four and six discs are placed in the jukebox, and the desired disc is accessed by a software program. Some jukeboxes can hold up to 100 discs. It is important to note, however, that only a few discs can be accessed at a given time. Jukeboxes are not recommended for workstations with multiple users who need simultaneous access to several different discs.

Multi-disc Tower Players

A multi-disc tower player houses several CD-ROM drives that can be accessed simultaneously, making these players popular on CD-ROM networks. Some of the tower players provide only two drives, while others may have as many as 64 drives. Before purchasing a tower player, be sure that your file server has enough controller cards (ports) to support it.

Purchasing a CD-ROM Drive

Buying a CD-ROM drive is becoming increasingly complex. In addition to price, there are many issues to consider, such as access time, data transfer rate, buffer size, and compatibility.

Access Time. CD-ROM drives are considerably slower than hard drives. One of the factors that affects the speed of the drives is the *access time*. The access time (or *seek time*) is the number of milliseconds that it takes the laser beam to move into position and locate the desired information on the disc. When investigating the access time, the smaller the better. A standard access time a few months ago was 700 milliseconds (ms); rates of less than 200 ms are available now. (Many hard drives have access times of 10 to 17 ms.) Fast access times are particularly important in applications such as databases, because the drive is constantly searching for new information.

Data Transfer Rate. Another important factor in the speed of a CD-ROM drive is the sustained *data transfer rate*—how fast the information is transferred from the disc to the host computer. The data transfer rate is measured in kilobytes per second (K/sec). In this case, a larger number is better. For example, the original audio compact discs had a transfer rate of 150 K/sec. This rate is commonly referred to as *single speed*. Many drives can now increase the data transfer rate by spinning the drive faster—either two, three, or four times faster. A double speed CD-ROM drive provides a data transfer rate of 300 K/sec; triple speed is 450 K/sec; and quad speed is 600 K/sec.

Buffer Size. The size of a memory buffer can also affect the speed of a CD-ROM drive. On some CD-ROM drives, a *memory buffer* stores information from the disc and sends it to the computer in high-speed bursts. Memory buffers can increase the performance of the application by increasing the rate at which information reaches the computer for processing. Current buffer sizes range from zero to 256K—the bigger the number, the better.

CD-Audio Controls. Almost all CD-ROM players can play audio compact discs. In many cases, audio discs must be controlled by software on the computer; however, some CD-ROM players provide control options for audio. These controls are convenient if you want to use the player for stand-alone audio without using the computer. Additional audio features to look for on CD-ROM players are headphone jacks and audio connectors for speakers.

Internal vs. External. CD-ROM drives are common in both internal and external configurations. Internal players are often less expensive and provide greater security from theft. The audio output from internal drives feeds directly into a sound card (such as Sound Blaster), leaving the input on the sound card free for other sources. External drives are easier to move from computer to computer, and they often provide additional external controls.

SCSI vs. Proprietary Controller. CD-ROM drives for MS-DOS computers require a controller—a place to plug the drive into the computer. Some CD-ROM drives are sold with a controller card and interface cable. These cards are referred to as proprietary, meaning they will work with only a specific CD-ROM drive.

Many of the current CD-ROM drives do not provide proprietary cards; instead, they work with SCSI or SCSI-2 controllers. This means that they can plug into an existing SCSI port on a computer or sound card. If you have a choice, the SCSI connections are generally a little faster than the proprietary interfaces. SCSI connections are also popular because they enable more than one device to be connected to the same port. For example, you can *daisychain* several CD-ROM drives to the same SCSI port by connecting them to each other (See fig. 2.3).

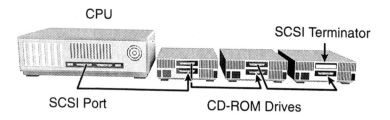

Fig. 2.3. CD-ROMs daisychained to a SCSI port.

Mean Time Between Failures (MTBF). Many advertisements for CD-ROM drives include a rating for the *mean time between failures* (MTBF). This number estimates how many hours the drive will last before it requires maintenance. A large number (such as 50,000 hours) is preferable.

Photo-CD Compatibility. Many CD-ROM drives are compatible with Kodak's standard for Photo-CD. This technology enables you to store 35mm slides or pictures on a compact disc. The cost of this storage can be as low as $2 per photo, and up to 100 photos can be saved to the Photo-CD disc in several separate sessions. You can view the Photo-CD with a special Kodak Photo-CD player or with any Photo-CD compatible CD-ROM player. Five different resolutions of each picture are stored on the disc.

If your CD-ROM drive is compatible with Photo-CD, you can import photographs into programs such as *PhotoShop* by Adobe Systems for editing. CD-ROM drives that are compatible with Photo-CD are either *single-session* or *multi-session*. A single-session drive can read only the first photographic session on the disc. The multi-session drives can read and display all of the photographs on the disc, whether they were placed on the disc during the first session or subsequent sessions. For example, if you took pictures of an office party in December and had the photos transferred to Photo-CD, you could later add pictures of a presentation in June. If your CD-ROM player were single-session, you would only be able to view the pictures of the party; if the player were multi-session, you could view all of the pictures on the disc.

Kodak has expanded Photo-CD technology and introduced several additional products. Interactivity is available through Photo-CD Portfolio. This product includes interactive branching and can mix photos, sounds, and text for "slide show" presentations. The pictures on Photo-CD Portfolio are stored at a lower resolution than Photo-CD; therefore, you can include up to 800 photos, rather than 100.

Caddy. Another consideration when comparing CD-ROM drives is whether or not they require a caddy for the disc. Disc caddies can help protect the disc from scratches, especially if the discs will be changed often. However, some people prefer drives that do not require a caddy because it is easier to load and unload the discs.

Software Caching Programs. Software caching programs use a computer's RAM to save information read from a CD-ROM disc. If the application requires information that has already been stored in RAM, the access time is much faster than reading directly from the CD-ROM. Software caching programs used in conjunction with CD-ROM drives can greatly improve the performance of the CD-ROM application—even though the actual speed of the CD-ROM drive has not changed.

Creating a CD-ROM Disc

Many industrial, military, and educational institutions produce custom CD-ROMs by recording the disc with a CD-Recorder or by sending the data to a mastering studio. Usually these applications focus on the dissemination of documentation (such as technical manuals), multimedia training programs, or internal databases.

The attractions of publishing a CD-ROM are apparent: the storage space on each disc is enormous, the "printing" cost is much less than either paper or diskettes, and the product can be searched rapidly and electronically. Although the exact procedure for mastering a CD-ROM will vary based on the application, several steps are common to most CD-ROM projects:

Step 1: Obtain the hardware

In order to create a CD-ROM, you must have a computer with the capacity to hold the volume of data required to run the application (up to 650 MB). The processing speed of the computer and a number of other factors are also important if you plan to record the CD-ROM in-house, because the information must be sent to the CD-Recorder in a steady stream. If the data stream is interrupted, the CD-ROM disc will be useless.

If you plan to send the data to a mastering studio, you must have a method for transporting the information to an external service bureau. The options for transporting the data include tape backups, removable magneto-optical drives, or large external disks.

Step 2: Gather the data

A major step in creating a CD-ROM is determining what information you are going to put on the disc. Basically, anything that can be stored in digital form can be included in a CD-ROM application; most of the applications center around large collections of text or multimedia. Although 600+ megabytes may seem like a lot of information, when you begin to add video and sound to an application, you can quickly exceed that limit.

The content of a CD-ROM often hinges on whether or not the data is already in digital form and whether you own the copyrights. Other considerations include the profile of the target audience and the computer systems available to the users. If the disc is being created as a commercial venture, the potential return on investment must also be analyzed. Issues such as the cost of obtaining copyright releases can easily impact profit.

Step 3: Convert the data into digital form

In the best of all worlds, the required information would already be digital, and you could skip this step. But chances are you will have to convert some of the data. The conversion process could mean using a scanner to capture images, digitizing video with a digitizing card, or using OCR (optical character recognition) software to convert text to digital form. Although all of these processes can be done in-house with the appropriate hardware and personnel, many companies choose to send the material to an outside contractor for conversion.

Step 4: Index the data

Indexing makes the information in CD-ROM databases accessible. The indexes enable the retrieval software to quickly access the desired information in specific records or fields. To facilitate the indexing process, codes or tags are often included in the text files.

There is a wide variety of indexing and retrieval software available (See "CD-ROM Resources" at the end of this chapter). The software you select depends on the nature of the data, the types of searches desired (keyword, proximity, wildcards, logical connectors, etc.), the limitations of the hardware, and the price. It is important to note that some software indexing companies require licensing fees based on a per-disc or per-application figure.

Step 5: Format the data

Before the information can be recorded on the CD-ROM, it must be formatted to one of the CD-ROM standards—usually either ISO 9660 (International Standards Organization) or Apple HFS (Hierarchical File System). ISO 9660 is the international standard that emerged from the original High Sierra format. Discs that are formatted with ISO 9660 can be read on MS-DOS, UNIX, and Macintosh computers if the appropriate retrieval software is present. To achieve cross-platform flexibility, the ISO 9660 requires strict adherence to file-naming and directory conventions.

The Apple HFS standard is used to create Macintosh-only CD-ROMs. This standard is the same file format used on all Macintosh floppy disks and hard disks. To produce a CD-ROM in HFS format, a hard drive is prepared with the files, icons, and windows adjusted to appear exactly the way you want the users to see the information on the CD-ROM. (It is best to format or de-fragment the drive first.) The views (name, icon, date, etc.) you select are the ones every user will see; therefore, you should choose the views carefully and check the positions and sizes of each window.

Software is available to format information into ISO 9660, HFS, or any of the specialized standards that have emerged in the industry, such as CD-Audio, CD-ROM XA, Photo-CD, CD-i, or 3DO formats.

Step 6: Premaster and test the data

Premastering arranges information in blocks and adds the appropriate file structure information. Software for premastering is available separately or may be combined with the formatting software. Many companies elect to send data to a service bureau for premastering and testing (See "CD-ROM Resources" at the end of this chapter).

Before the final disc is produced, it is wise to test the application. In many cases, a simulation is set up on the target computer hardware. A large hard drive or magneto-optical disc can be used for the simulation along with special software that adjusts the timing of the simulation disk to that of a CD-ROM drive. An alternative to simulation with a hard drive is to create a CD-Recordable disc for test purposes.

Step 7: Master the CD-ROM

There are two primary choices for recording a custom CD-ROM: You can use a CD-Recordable (CD-R) drive, or you can send your files to a professional replicator. If you are making only a handful of CDs for each application, it is more cost-efficient to record them yourself with a CD-R system. If you need more than 30 discs for each application, a professional replication service may be the best choice, because they can record a master disc and make copies quickly and inexpensively.

Professional Replication

The cost of disc production and replication through a commercial company includes a fixed fee for the master ($500-$1,000) and a per-disc charge for the duplicates (about $2 per disc, depending on the quantity). If the replicator creates the premaster, an additional fee (about $125/hour) will be included.

To produce the copies, a master disc serves as the first generation of the duplication process. When selecting a mastering facility, ensure that they will do extensive data error verification and correction. Remember, after the disc is pressed, it cannot be changed.

CD-Recordables

If you only need a few copies of each title, or if you want to test a prototype of your application before creating a master disc, it makes sense to use a CD-Recordable drive. The cost of these drives has decreased dramatically in the past few years (to about $3,000). A blank CD-R disc costs about $15, and the quality is equal to that of a replicated disc. Hardware is an important issue when producing a CD-R disc. In order to create an error-free disc, the information must be transferred in a steady stream from the hard drive to the CD-R drive. After the software is formatted and the hardware is configured, the procedure is as easy as clicking "record."

CD-ROM Networks

Several computers can share a CD-ROM drive if the appropriate hardware and software are connected to a network (See chapter 5 for more information about networks). With a CD-ROM drive on a network, the applications can be accessed throughout a building or group of buildings; however, CD-ROMs on a network can be quite slow if the demand is high. Copyright issues must also be considered. Be sure to obtain a network-ready, multiple-user license for each application.

Another issue to consider with networked CD-ROMs is multimedia support. In many cases, sound will play only at the server station, not the individual workstations. In addition, video and animation files can be slow and jerky over a network.

There are three basic approaches for implementing a CD-ROM network: peer-to-peer, a combination file server/CD-ROM server, and a dedicated CD-ROM server. Each of these approaches has advantages and disadvantages depending on the security required and the administrative support available.

Peer-to-Peer

In a peer-to-peer network, there is no file server. Instead, a small group of computers is connected to each other, and software allows them to share their resources. Peer-to-peer networking is inexpensive and easy to install. Simply put a network card in each machine, connect them with cables, and install the peer-to-peer software.

CD-ROM drives can be connected to every computer on the peer-to-peer network, or they can be connected to only one or two computers, for all to share. Peer-to-peer networks are most appropriate when the simultaneous demand for CD-ROM access is low and when the response times are not critical (See chapter 5 for more information on peer-to-peer networks).

Combination File Server/CD-ROM Server

Another option for networking CD-ROMs is to attach a CD-ROM player (or several players) to an existing file server. This approach offers better performance and tighter control than the peer-to-peer option, but it also requires more ongoing management. Other factors that may impact a combination file server/CD-ROM server configuration are:

- the amount of use the file server already supports
- the number of free expansion slots on the server
- the amount of RAM on the file server
- the availability of personnel to swap CD-ROM discs

Dedicated CD-ROM Server

A third option for CD-ROM networking is a dedicated server for CD-ROM. Multiple CD-ROM servers can be placed on a network, making hundreds of CD-ROM drives accessible to users without affecting other file server operations. Dedicated servers offer excellent security and management.

Advantages and Disadvantages of CD-ROM

Although CD-ROM technology offers many benefits, it is not appropriate for every situation. The following are some of the benefits and limitations of CD-ROM technology for business, industry, and education.

Advantages of CD-ROM

Storage capacity. Each CD-ROM disc can hold over 650 megabytes of data, graphics, video, and sound. This is equivalent to hundreds of floppy disks and more than an entire printed encyclopedia.

Portability. CD-ROM discs are small and lightweight, making them an ideal medium for transporting data. Portable CD-ROM players are helping to revolutionize sales and maintenance processes; it is not unusual for salespeople and technicians to carry all of their reference information in a lightweight, easy-to-use unit.

Durability. CD-ROM discs are encased in plastic and are very durable. Although they should be handled with care, fingerprints and slight scratches will not usually impair their performance. In addition, the discs are read with a laser beam, so there is no direct contact or wear on the disc as it is played.

Unaffected by magnetic fields. Because CD-ROM discs are optical, they will not be accidentally erased if they are X-rayed or exposed to a magnetic field.

Low cost of replication. Once a master has been created, CD-ROMs are very inexpensive to reproduce.

Cross-Platform. If the information on the disc is formatted in the ISO 9660 standard, it can be read by a Macintosh, MS-DOS, or UNIX computer. This cross-platform flexibility reduces the cost of producing, stocking, and selling products on CD-ROM.

Networkable. Information from a CD-ROM can be accessed by multiple users via local or wide area networks.

Availability of titles. The number of CD-ROM titles has increased exponentially. Several thousand commercial titles are now available.

Speed. Decreasing the time it takes to access information can be a key competitive and educational advantage. CD-ROM technology provides access to a large quantity of searchable information. Although the access time of CD-ROM drives is slower than that of hard drives, the speed of the search time compared to manual methods is very impressive.

Decreased software pirating. Because most CD-ROMs contain several hundred megabytes of integrated data, there is a decreased likelihood that the applications will be pirated and copied to a hard drive.

Disadvantages of CD-ROM

Read only. CD-ROMs cannot be updated or changed in any way.

Slow access time. When compared to hard drives, CD-ROM drives are relatively slow. It takes about 10 times longer to access information with a single speed CD-ROM than it does with a hard drive. Depending on the number of users, access on a network can be frustrating.

Slow data transfer rates. The data transfer rate from a CD-ROM to a computer is slow. This limitation affects the display of complex graphics and digital movies.

Lack of standards for retrieval software. There is very little consistency among CD-ROM applications. For example, in one application, the Help function may be accessed with the F1 key; in another application, the Help command may be Control + H. Techniques for using wildcards and logical connectors also vary widely from application to application.

Installation. Installation of the hardware is generally straightforward. However, installing the software can be a frustrating experience. In the MS-DOS environment, two files must be changed to allow the computer to access the CD-ROM (autoexec.bat and config.sys). Although most install programs modify these two files automatically, there may be conflicts with other applications. In the Macintosh environment, the proper files must be placed in the system folder, and the correct versions of the system finder are required.

Compact Disc Standards

Over the years, several standards have evolved to define the format in which compact discs are recorded. These standards do not, however, ensure compatibility between the various technologies, and many of the formats require a specific player. A brief overview of several of the standards is provided in this section, as well as a chart that defines some of the relationships (See fig. 2.4). Note that many of the standards may also be referred to by a color; this terminology was established to help differentiate the formats.

Compact Disc-Audio (CD-Audio). Compact Disc-Audio, or Red Book, was the first standard for storing digital information on compact discs. CD-Audio discs store a maximum of 74 minutes of high-quality audio (usually music) on a compact disc. Almost all of the other formats (CD-ROM, CD-i, etc.) can play CD-Audio discs (See chapter 4 for more information about CD-Audio).

Compact Disc-Read Only Memory (CD-ROM). CD-ROM discs store a combination of digital text, graphics, sound, and video. They are recorded in the Yellow Book standard, which can be formatted in a variety of file structures, including Apple HFS and ISO 9660.

Compact Disc-Recordable (CD-R). You can record data on a CD-R disc, but you cannot erase it. CD-R discs, or Orange Book, are gold in color, compatible with CD-ROM, and can be played on regular CD-ROM players. (Note: CD-R is sometimes referred to as CD-WO for Compact Disc-Write Once.)

Compact Disc-Interactive (CD-i). CD-i, or Green Book, is a hardware and software specification for an interactive audio, video, and computer system based on compact discs as the storage media. The output from CD-i displays on a standard television set. CD-i has a wide range of capabilities and is aimed at the consumer market where low cost is important (See chapter 3 for more information on CD-i).

3DO. 3DO is similar to CD-i. It is a multimedia player that connects to a television set. 3DO was released in 1993 and targets the game and consumer markets (See chapter 3 for more information on 3DO).

Photographic Compact Disc (Photo-CD). Photo CD was developed by Kodak to store photographic images on compact discs. The compact disc is played on a special Photo-CD player (or compatible player such as CD-i or CD-ROM XA) and displayed on a television set. Many CD-ROM players have the ability to display Photo-CD discs. Photo-CDs are produced on a recordable player and adhere to the Orange Book format.

Video-CD. Compact discs designed to deliver full-motion video are called Video-CDs or White Book. These discs can store up to 74 minutes of video, but they require special video decoder hardware. CD-i and 3DO drives can be upgraded to play Video-CD (See chapter 3 for more information on Video-CD).

Figure 2.4 illustrates the compatibility among the common compact disc formats. For example, all of the players listed (CD-Audio, CD-ROM, CD-i, and 3DO) can play CD-Audio discs, but only the 3DO player can play 3DO discs.

Player \ Format	CD-Audio	CD-ROM	CD-R	CD-i	3DO	Photo-CD	Video-CD
CD-Audio	Yes	No	No	No	No	No	No
CD-ROM	Yes	Yes	Yes	No	No.	Yes	No
CD-i	Yes	No	No	Yes	No	Yes	Yes
3DO	Yes	No	No	No	Yes	Yes	Yes

Fig. 2.4. Compatibility of common formats.

Mixed Mode CD-ROM. Mixed mode CD-ROMs contain both computer data and CD-Audio tracks. The computer data is recorded on the inner tracks of the disc, and the audio is recorded on the outer tracks. This configuration allows more versatility. However, because the player can only read one part of the disc at a time, the discs must be planned carefully to avoid unexpected interruptions as the program switches from data to sound.

Compact Disc-Read Only Memory eXtended Architecture (CD-ROM XA). CD-ROM XA (also referred to as Yellow Book: Mode 2) interleaves, or mixes, the audio and the graphics/text on the compact disc. With this format, audio can be played at the same time that graphics or text are being displayed. CD-ROM XA provides seamless multimedia applications without depending on large hard drives or RAM caches.

CD+G. Some audio CDs have a small amount of graphic information encoded on the disc. With an appropriate player (e.g., CD-i), you can view the graphics while listening to the music. If these discs are played in a regular audio compact disc player, the graphics will not be displayed.

Write Once-Read Many (WORM). Most compact disc technologies are "read-only." WORM refers to a technology that can record (but not erase) a compact disc. WORM discs are not compatible with most CD-ROM drives, so they are becoming less popular than CD-R discs. Although WORM discs can hold more information than CD-ROM discs, the drives are much more expensive.

Conclusion

CD-ROM technology has established a strong base in business, industry, and academia because of its large storage capacity, durability, and low cost. CD-ROMs provide almost instant access to over 650 megabytes of text, graphics, video, and sound. Trends in CD-ROM technology include continually decreasing costs of hardware, the availability of inexpensive CD-ROM Recordable drives, and a proliferation of other similar, but generally incompatible, technologies for delivering multimedia on a compact disc.

CD-ROM Resources

Guides and Directories

CD-ROM Buyer's Guide and Handbook, 462 Danbury Road, Wilton, CT 06897, 800-248-8466

CD-ROM Directory, 462 Danbury Road, Wilton, CT 06897, 800-248-8466

CD-ROM Facts and Figures, 462 Danbury Road, Wilton, CT 06897, 800-248-8466

CD-ROMs in Print, 11 Ferry Lane West, Westport, CT 06880, 203-226-6967

For information on the trends and sales of CD-ROM, contact:

Dataquest, 408-437-8316

Digital Information Group, 203-348-2751

Freeman Associates, 805-963-3853

Infotech, 802-457-4728

Optical Publishing Association, 614-442-8805

SIMBA/Communications Trends, 203-834-0033

Software Publishers Association, 202-452-1600

Titles Referenced in the Text

Compton's Multimedia Encyclopedia, Compton's New Media, 2320 Camino Vida Roble, Carlsbad, CA 92009, 619-929-2626

Computer Select, Ziff Communications Co., 1 Park Avenue, New York, NY 10016, 212-503-4400

CorelDRAW! Corel Corporation, 1600 Carling Avenue, Ottawa, Ontario K1Z 8R7, 613-728-8200

Mayo Clinic Family Health Book, Interactive Ventures, Inc., 1330 Corporate Center Curve #305, Eagan, MN 55121, 507-282-2076

Microsoft Encarta Multimedia Encyclopedia, Microsoft Corporation, One Microsoft Way, Redmond, WA 98052, 800-426-9400

National Economic, Social and Environmental DataBank, U.S. Department of Commerce, Room H-4885, Washington, DC 20230, 202-482-1986

New Grolier Multimedia Encyclopedia, Grolier Electronic Publishing Inc., Sherman Turnpike, Danbury, CT 06816, 203-797-3500

PC-SIG Library, PC-SIG, 1030-D East Duane Avenue, Sunnyvale, CA 94086, 800-245-6717

PhotoShop, Adobe Systems, 1585 Charleston Road, Mountain View, CA 94039, 800-833-6687

ProPhone, ProCD, Inc., 8 Doaks Lane, Little Harbor, Marblehead, MA 01945, 617-631-9200

Sherlock Holmes, ICOM Simulations, Inc., 648 S. Wheeling Road, Wheeling, IL 60090, 708-520-4440

Street Atlas USA, Delorme Publishing Company Inc., Lower Main Street, Freeport, ME 04032, 800-227-1656

CD-ROM Drives

Apple Computer, 20525 Mariani Avenue, Cupertino, CA 95014, 408-996-1010

Chinon America, 615 Hawaii Avenue, Torrance, CA 90503, 800-441-0222

Hitachi Multimedia Systems, 401 W. Artesia B1, Compton, CA 90220, 800-369-0422

Mitsumi Electronics, 4655 Old Ironsides Drive, Santa Clara, CA 95054, 408-970-0700

NEC Technologies, 1255 Michael Drive, Wood Dale, IL 60191, 800-632-4636

Panasonic Communications, Two Panasonic Way, Secaucus, NJ 07094, 800-742-8086

Philips Consumer Electronics, One Philips Drive, Knoxville, TN 37914, 800-835-3506

Pioneer New Media, 2265 E. 220th Street, Long Beach, CA 90810, 800-444-6784

Plextor, 4255 Burton Drive, Santa Clara, CA 95054, 408-980-1838

Sony Computer Products, 3300 Zanker Road, San Jose, CA 95134, 800-352-7669

Toshiba America, 9740 Irvine Boulevard, Irvine, CA 92718, 714-457-0777

Wearnes Technology, 1015 E. Brokaw Road, San Jose, CA 95131, 408-456-8838

CD-ROM Recording Hardware and Software

CD-ROM Strategies (Software), 6 Venture Street, Irvine, CA 92718, 714-453-1702

DataDisc (Software), Route 3, Box 1108, Gainesville, VA 22065, 800-328-2347

Dataware (Software), 222 3rd Street, Cambridge, MA 02142, 800-229-2222

Eastman Kodak Company (Hardware/software), 343 State Street, Rochester, NY 14650, 800-242-2424

Elektroson (Software), 10 Presidential Boulevard, Cynwood, PA 19004, 215-695-8444

Incat Systems (Software), One Faneuil Hall Marketplace, Boston, MA 02109, 508-443-5950

Information Management Research (Software), 5660 Greenwood Plaza Boulevard, Englewood, CO 80111, 303-689-0022

JVC Information Products (Hardware/software), 19900 Beach Boulevard, Huntington Beach, CA 92648, 714-965-2610

Knowledge Access (Software), 2685 Marine Way, Mountain View, CA 94043, 415-969-0606

Meridian Data (Hardware/software), 5615 Scotts Valley Drive, Scotts Valley, CA 95066, 800-767-2537

MicroRetrieval Corporation (Software), 101 Main Street, Cambridge, MA 02142, 617-577-1574

Optical Media International (Software), 180 Knowles Drive, Los Gatos, CA 95030, 800-347-2664

Optimage Interactive Services (Software), 1501 50th Street, West Des Moines, Iowa 50266, 515-225-7000

Philips (Hardware/software), 20720 S. Leapwood Avenue, Carson, CA 90746, 800-835-3506

Pinnacle Micro (Hardware/software), 19 Technology Drive, Irvine, CA 92718, 800-553-7070

Ricoh (Hardware), 3001 Orchard Parkway, San Jose, CA 95134, 408-432-8800

Rimage (Hardware/software), 7725 Washington Avenue S., Minneapolis, MN 55439, 800-445-8288

Sony Corporation (Hardware/software), 33 Zanker, San Jose, CA 95134, 800-654-8802

TMS, Inc. (Software), 110 W. Third Street, Stillwater, OK 74076, 405-377-0880

Trace (Software), 1040 E. Brokaw, San Jose, CA 95131, 408-437-3380

Yamaha Corporation (Hardware), 981 Ridder Park Drive, San Jose, CA 95131, 408-437-3133

Young Minds (Hardware/software), P.O. Box 6910, Redlands, CA 92375, 909-335-1350

CD-ROM Mastering Plants

3M Software Media & CD-ROM, Building 223-5South, St. Paul, MN 55144-1000, 800-364-3577

Digital Audio Disc Corporation, 1800 North Freitridge Avenue, Terre Haute, IN 47804, 812-466-6821

DMI, 1409 Foulk Road, Suite 202, Wilmington, DE 19803, 302-433-2500

METATEC, 7001 Discovery Boulevard, Dublin, OH 43017, 614-761-2000

Nimbus Information Systems, Box 7305, Charlottesville, VA 22906, 800-782-0778

Optical Disc Corporation, 12150 Mora Drive, Santa Fe Springs, CA 90670, 310-946-3050

Optical Media International, 485 Alberto Way, Los Gatos, CA 95032, 408-395-4332

SONY Electronic Publishing, 1800 N. Fruitridge Avenue, Terre Haute, IN 47803, 812-462-8160

Recommended Reading

Apple Computer Inc. 1992. *Apple CD-ROM handbook: A guide to planning, creating and producing a CD-ROM*. Reading, MA: Addison-Wesley.

Barron, D. 1994. Reading, 'riting, and recording: Master your own CD-ROMs. *PC Graphics & Video*, 3(1): 17-23.

Beheshti, J., and A. Large. 1992. Networking CD-ROMs: Response time implications. *CD-ROM Professional* 5(11): 70-77.

Bell, S. J. 1993. Providing remote access to CD-ROMs: Some practical advice. *CD-ROM Professional* 6(1): 43-47.

Benford, T. 1994. Double-speed CD-ROM drives. *CD-ROM Today*, 2(2): 37-42.

Berger, P., and S. Kinnel. 1994. Which one should I buy? Evaluating CD-ROMs. *Multimedia Schools*, 1(1): 21-28.

Bernard, B. 1992. The process of CD-ROM publishing: A guide for print publishers. *The Seybold Report on Desktop Publishing*, 6(12): 9(6).

Biedny, D. 1993. Bake your own CDs: From recipe to reality. *NewMedia*, 3(8): 65-73.

Bishop, P. 1993. In-house CD-ROMs becoming serious business. *MacWEEK Special Report: CD-ROM Publishing*, 7(27): 38(2).

Blass, B. 1994. Buyers' guide: 31 multi-speed CD-ROM drives. *Multimedia World*, 1(4): 74-70.

Bosak, S. 1993. The NetWare CD-ROM solution. *BYTE*, 18(13): 151-52.

Brannon, C. 1993. Sharing the wealth: How to create a CD-ROM network with Windows for Workgroups. *CD-ROM Today*, 1(1): 42-45.

———. 1993. Speedy CDs: 4 caches that optimize your CD-ROM drive. *CD-ROM Today*, 1(2): 31-38.

———. 1994. Getting started with Kodak Photo CD. *CD-ROM Today*, 1(3): 33-36.

Churbuck, D. C. 1994, January. Lights! camera! manual! *Forbes*, 153: 92(2).

Data Distribution Laboratory 1993. Premastering and CD-WO software for the PC: Evaluations of the top in-house publishing software. *CD-ROM Professional* 6(3): 34-49.

Dataware Technologies, Inc. 1993. *Guide to CD-ROM and multimedia publishing*. Cambridge, MA: Dataware Technologies.

Eiser, L. 1993. Shopping for a CD-ROM drive. *Technology & Learning* 13(7): 40-46.

Halfhill, T. R. 1993. Kodak's Photo CD Portfolio: The new family album? *CD-ROM Today*, 1(1): 112.

Holsinger, E. 1994, June. Make your own CD-ROMs. *MacUser*. 101-7.

Jerram, P. 1994. CD-ROM titles explosion. *NewMedia*, 4(6): 40-46.

Johnson, H. 1993. Writeable CD-ROM is not for everyone. *Computer Digest*, 8(6): 17-19.

Karney, J. 1994. Sharing a CD-ROM. *PC Magazine*, 13(4): 171-78.

Kittle, P. 1992. Networking the light fantastic—CD-ROMs on LANs. *CD-ROM Professional* 5(1): 30-37.

Magel, M. 1994, February. CD-ROM masters & one-off options. *Multimedia Producer*, S-9.

McQueen, H. 1993. CD-ROM servers: An overview. *CD-ROM Professional* 6(9): 54-57.

Parker, D. J. 1993. A rainbow of standards. *CD-ROM Professional* 6(3): 151-54.

Quain, J. R., and C. Ellison. 1993, December. Honey, I shrunk the library! *Home Office Computing*, 11: 106(6).

Reveaux, T. 1994. The players the players play. *NewMedia*, 4(1): 55-57.

Rugg, R. 1993. Installing a low-cost LAN—Fool-proof tips from a pro. *CD-ROM Professional* 6(9): 114-18.

Schultz, D. A. 1993. So you want to publish a CD-ROM—Practical tips and hard-won advice. *CD-ROM Professional* 6(1): 50-53.

Soto, S. 1993, November. Planning for a CD-ROM drive purchase. *Computer Digest*, 19.

Spanbauer, S. 1993. The write stuff: CD-Recordable. *NewMedia* 3(10): 62-68.

Starr, K. 1993. The building blocks of a CD-ROM local area network. *CD-ROM Professional* 6(1): 65-67.

Strauss, R. 1994. Budgeting and scheduling a CD-ROM project. *NewMedia*, 4(2): 99-101.

Thiel, T. J. 1993. Costs of CD-ROM production—What they are and how to overcome them. *CD-ROM Professional*, 6(2): 43-46.

Thompson, T. 1994, March. Budget CD recording. *BYTE*, 145-47.

Udell, J. 1993. Start the presses: CD-ROM publishing comes to the desktop. *BYTE*, 18(2): 116-34.

Victor, T. 1993. From digits to disc. *CD-ROM Today*, 1(1): 24-29.

———. 1993. The evolving world of CD-ROM formats: CD-ROM/XA and multi-session bound to be the very next phase. *CD-ROM Today*, 1(2): 63-66.

Worthington, P. 1993, November. Corporate compact discs. *PCWorld*, 11: 15.

3

Video Technologies

A Scenario

Satomi had spent the last several days down on the factory floor with a camcorder; collecting video footage. The new computerized metal lathe was scheduled to go online within a month, and a lot of training had to take place between now and then. The manufacturer of the lathe had supplied some generic video of the lathe in operation at another factory, but her factory installation had several important differences.

The final phase of training for the lathe operators would take place on the actual equipment, but there was a large number of employees involved and very little time. Satomi had decided several weeks ago that training time on the new lathe would be most efficient if she cycled the trainees through a preliminary multimedia course that combined the features presented by the manufacturer's tape with the custom features required for her factory. In addition, she decided to digitize the video so that it could be delivered to all of the workstations in the factory through the local area network. She also decided to make the program interactive and include embedded questions to test each trainee on the essential safety procedures.

Satomi's initial efforts went toward putting together a computer-based training program of the basic instructional and evaluative components she needed to teach her students. With the permission of the manufacturer and the help of her engineers, she then selected, digitized, and inserted video clips from the generic videotape into the computer program.

Next Satomi selected the best scenes from her video of the factory floor and digitized them. She added some voice-over narration from one of the engineers to explain a key point, and then inserted the video clips into the multimedia training program.

Following review by the manufacturer's representative and her engineers, Satomi would make any needed revisions on the computer. After that, the program would be copied to a recordable CD-ROM, and installed on the company's CD-ROM server. Employees would be able to view the training program from their workstations, and records would indicate when each employee had completed the preliminary training and was ready to practice on the new lathe.

* * * *

The visual realism offered by video technology has been an important component of instruction since the debut of television and videotape. Videodisc technology has been used for military and industrial training since the 1970s. More recently, this technology has become popular for educational applications, because it offers an inexpensive way to display high-quality, full-screen video.

The current trend in multimedia instruction is to digitize the video and deliver it via computer. Digital video offers many possibilities for desktop video editing, interactive training stored on compact discs, and video teleconferencing. This chapter examines the video technology trends and includes:

- An overview of videodisc formats and terminology

- Advantages and disadvantages of videodiscs

- Videodisc applications for training

- Steps for creating a videodisc master

- Configurations for video delivery

- Advantages and disadvantages of digital video

- Procedures for digitizing video

- Guidelines for selecting a video digitizing card

- An overview of DVI, QuickTime, Video for Windows, CD-i, 3DO, Video-CD, and HDTV

Introduction to Videodisc Technology

When television was in its developmental stage in the 1940s, the video display and broadcast standards for the United States were developed by the National Television Standards Committee (NTSC). The NTSC standard specifies that 525 horizontal lines are scanned on the monitor for each frame (picture) and that 30 frames are displayed every second. Each video frame consists of two fields; the first field is produced when the odd-numbered lines are scanned, and scanning the even-numbered lines creates the second field. The rapid display of the frames creates the illusion of movement.

When videotape is recorded, the signals for the scan lines are stored as magnetic pulses. A videodisc stores the signals for the scan lines optically on a hard plastic disc rather than magnetically on a tape. It is important to note that although videodisc is an optical medium, it produces a standard analog NTSC signal when it is played.

Videodisc Formats

Videodiscs are either eight or 12 inches in diameter and may be recorded in one of two formats. The Constant Angular Velocity (CAV) format has a capacity for 30 minutes of motion video on each side of the disc (54,000 still frames) and the ability to still frame (stop on one frame). Each frame on a CAV videodisc has a unique number assignment (from 1-54,000), and each frame can be instantly accessed with a remote control unit, barcode reader, or computer. The CAV videodisc is the most popular format for education and training because of its versatility.

The other videodisc format is Constant Linear Velocity (CLV). A CLV disc is the same size as a CAV disc, but the video frames are stored in a different configuration. Instead of having one frame on each concentric circle, a CLV disc may have several frames and parts of frames on the same circle. CLV discs can store 60 minutes of video on each side, but they cannot stop and display a single frame. Most CLV discs are used for movies or linear programs. Instead of frame numbers, CLV discs are accessed by time codes.

Levels of Interactivity

Videodisc programs are often called interactive videodisc because the user can selectively access segments or frames. Three levels of interactivity have been defined to indicate the amount of control the user has and the kinds of hardware or software required to achieve that control.

Level I. Level I interactivity is the level of control gained by using the videodisc player alone, without a computer connected to it. The disc access is controlled through the control panel on the player, a remote control unit, or a barcode reader. Level I interactivity is popular in schools because of the ease of operation and the fact that a computer connection is not required.

Level II. Level II videodiscs are also used without a computer, but the videodisc itself contains an embedded computer program. A processing unit inside the videodisc player loads and runs the program, and the user interacts through the remote control unit. Level II videodiscs are not very common because many videodisc players are not Level II compatible, and the computer program on the videodisc cannot be changed or updated.

Level III. Level III interactivity is generally considered the most flexible and interactive form of videodisc control because a computer is connected to the videodisc player. With Level III interactivity, the program can branch based on keyboard and other student inputs. Databases and other information can also be used in conjunction with the video images. Level III programs enable the computer to act as an instructional manager by storing student performances and records.

Advantages and Disadvantages of Videodisc Technology

Compared with videotape, videodiscs offer many advantages, but there are also some drawbacks to this technology. This section reviews the benefits and limitations of videodisc technology in comparison to videotape technology.

Advantages of Videodisc Technology

Random Access. All videodiscs are encoded with either frame numbers (CAV) or time code (CLV). By using a remote control unit, barcode reader, or computer, users can access the desired frames of the disc quickly and accurately. Many discs have chapter stops to enable rapid access to predetermined sections of the disc.

Fast seek time. Videotapes may require ten minutes or more to reach the beginning or end of a tape. With a videodisc, the seek time is measured in seconds. Very slow players may require up to five seconds to move from the first to the last frame of the disc; fast players can navigate the disc in less than a second.

Durability. Videodiscs are read optically, so there is no direct physical contact. Therefore, the estimated shelf life of a videodisc is much greater than that of a videotape. In addition, videodiscs are made of rugged plastic and are extremely durable.

Quality. Videodiscs provide a higher quality of picture because they can display over 350 lines of horizontal resolution. VHS videotapes can display only 200 to 250 lines of resolution.

Interactivity. Although it is possible to control videotape players with computers, it is much easier to control videodisc players. Most of the commercial model videodisc players have RS-232 ports on the back to connect a computer interface cable. Once connected, the computer can send commands, such as "play frames 12345 through 23455." The majority of the hypermedia authoring systems offer easy interface commands for videodiscs.

Still frame. It is difficult to pause a videotape to display a single frame unless you have a very high-end, commercial videotape player, and even then the tape may be stretched. Videodiscs can be halted on a still frame for hours with no damage. In fact, many videodiscs are designed to display separate static video images, rather than motion segments.

Multiple audio tracks. Two analog audio tracks are available on all videodiscs. In addition, many videodiscs provide two additional channels of digital audio.

Disadvantages of Videodisc Technology

Read only. Videodiscs are read only. After the disc is recorded, it cannot be changed. This constraint is one of the major reasons that videodisc technology has never had much impact on the home video market.

Cost of development. Production costs for the design and development of quality videodisc programs can be very high if professional actors and high-end equipment are used.

Cost of hardware. There are several variables that impact the price of commercial and consumer videodisc players. Commercial players that interface with computers and provide remote control units range between $700 to $2,000.

Maintenance costs. It is not unusual to spend several hundred dollars to repair a videodisc player, and it may be difficult to find a repair shop locally.

Lack of interface standards. Connecting a computer to a videodisc player can be frustrating. Different players require different software drivers and interface cables. In addition, the baud rates (speed of transmission) must be set correctly.

Limited motion sequences. Up to 54,000 still frames is a tremendous capacity for videodisc storage, but this only represents 30 minutes of motion video—much less motion than a videotape can store.

Videodisc Applications for Training

There are many different applications for videodisc technology in business, industry, and education. These applications include documentaries, information kiosks, point-of-sale systems, training programs, educational programs, and visual databases.

Documentaries and Movies. Videodiscs are excellent storage media for quality video footage. Many companies that produce documentaries find videodiscs to be the ideal means of delivery and distribution. There is an abundance of videodisc movies available commercially that provide low-cost, high-quality options to videotapes.

Information Kiosks. Videodiscs are commonly used in stand-alone kiosk systems designed to provide quick and easy information to people at malls, airports, or other public places. The objective of these systems is to provide travelers or shoppers guidance about which sites to see, restaurants to visit, or routes to travel. Some of the more sophisticated systems take advantage of the presentation power of videodisc technology and also provide computer capabilities to print maps or make reservations through telecommunications.

Point-of-Sale Systems. Videodiscs can also be used as electronic salespersons. For example, a mall or store may have a system that can display video images of a wide variety of sporting goods, clothing, or hard-to-stock merchandise. The customer uses the system to investigate the products and receives information such as price and availability. In some cases, the systems can also order the products for the customer and provide printed receipts.

Training Programs. Videodiscs have been used to provide visual and audio realism in military and industrial training for years. Most of these programs are created in-house or by a subcontractor. Videodisc training programs offer the benefits of audiovisual realism along with the management and database capabilities of a computer. Videodisc programs are especially appropriate for training when a large amount of full-screen, full-motion video is required, as in role-playing scenarios and procedures that require complex motion. Although most of the videodisc training programs are developed for custom programs, there are a few commercial applications for generic topics such as electronics and hazardous materials.

Educational Programs. The videodisc market for educational programs has exploded in the past few years. There are hundreds of videodisc programs available for students from preschool through college. These programs cover a wide range of topics, including simulations for science, tutorials for mathematics, and demonstrations of cartoon drawing. Some of the programs include sophisticated software, but the majority are Level I applications that include lesson plans and activities printed with barcodes.

Visual Databases. A *visual database* is a videodisc made up primarily of individual pictures. The images are designed to be displayed as still frames rather than played as motion. Because there can be up to 54,000 frames on a videodisc, visual databases can offer access to an enormous amount of visual material. Many companies use visual databases to produce catalogs and archive images.

Creating a Videodisc

Producing a videodisc is similar to creating a videotape. This section contains a step-by-step plan to create a videodisc program.

Step 1: Produce a Videotape (often called a premaster)

The first step in creating a videodisc is producing a videotape of the source material with timecodes. It is then converted to videodisc by a production house with a videodisc recorder. The quality of the videotape used to record the source material is important and directly proportional to the quality of the final videodisc. The best options for video formats are either Super VHS, 3/4 inch U-matic, 1 inch type C, broadcast quality Betacam, or digital tape.

The content of the video can include anything you can videotape, including motion, artwork, slides, and photographs. The only limit is that the final videotape cannot exceed 30 minutes in length. Probably the easiest source material to include is motion video, but remember, you are producing a videodisc, not a videotape, and one of its best features is the ability to display a still picture.

The videodisc production house will require that there be a standard color test signal, Color Bars, on the beginning of the videotape. There must also be an audio tone recorded on the tape over the color bars. Bars and tone should run for 1 minute 40 seconds, followed by 20 seconds of black without tone. You must also identify the time codes for the SAP (Start of Active Program) and EAP (End of Active Program) points on your tape (See fig. 3.1). These are the time code addresses of the first frame of video and the last frame of video you want to appear on the disc.

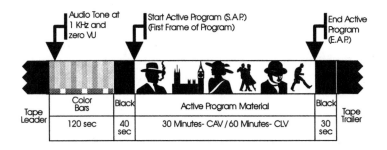

Fig. 3.1. Videotape format for videodisc premastering.

Step 2: Note Chapter and Picture Stops

Videodiscs designed for Level I interactivity usually include chapter and picture stops. A chapter stop is a frame on the disc that the player can "jump" to during a chapter search. A picture stop is a frame on the disc where the player will automatically stop and wait for the user to respond in some way. Picture stops are often placed on menu screens, where the disc will pause until the user makes a new selection. Level I videodiscs are often more demanding to design and produce than Level III videodiscs because the sequence of material on a Level I disc is critical.

A Level III videodisc is designed to be used with a computer that can randomly access any frame or sequence of frames. For a Level III videodisc, the material does not have to be recorded on the disc in the same sequence it is to be viewed, because the computer can jump to any point. Level III discs do not usually require chapter or picture stops because the computer controls the starting and stopping points on a disc.

After you have recorded the premaster tape, identify the chapter and picture stops by noting the specific time code "addresses." Provide a list of these addresses by time code to the production house when you submit your premaster tape. They will insert the chapter and picture stops as the videodisc is made. Most production houses will allow up to 50 chapter and picture stops per disc without an additional charge.

Step 3: Record Final Videodisc

There are several ways to produce the final videodisc. If numerous copies are going to be distributed, a recording studio will produce a "master" disc and then stamp copies from the master. The master generally costs about $1,800, and the copies about $18 each. This procedure provides top-quality, durable videodiscs.

If you only need a few videodiscs, another option is to record directly from the premaster videotape to a videodisc. Optical Disc Corporation (ODC) markets a direct-record, videodisc recorder that meets the laservision standards established by the International Electronic Commission. (Videodiscs that meet the laservision standard can play in any videodisc player.) ODC machines are available at a number of production houses and are used primarily to produce check discs (videodiscs used to check the content before the final disc is mastered). These plastic discs are quite durable and, with care, last a long time. The cost of these discs is usually between $250 and $300; more durable glass versions are available for around $500. (A list of videodisc production houses is included at the end of this chapter.)

Video Delivery Configurations

There are many consumer and commercial models of videodisc players on the market. The consumer models are designed to be used in a home—primarily to watch movies. These players have excellent sound quality and are often able to read both sides of a videodisc without turning it over. Consumer models are not generally designed to interface with a computer.

The commercial models are designed for interactive programs and are more expensive than the consumer models. Commercial videodisc players are designed to interface with laser barcode readers and computers to provide user control and interactivity.

The configuration for Level I interactivity consists of a video monitor and videodisc player, connected through audio and video cables. The configuration of Level III programs is a bit more complex, and has evolved over the last 15-20 years. The basic consideration has been that the video signal (NTSC) from the videodisc player is different from the computer signal (computer signals are also referred to as RGB because color is divided into three components—red, green, and blue). Without special hardware, the two signals are incompatible—the video monitor cannot display the computer signals, and the computer monitor cannot display the video.

Two Monitor Delivery

The earliest applications of interactive videodisc (and still the most common in schools) used two separate monitors—one for the video and one for the computer (See fig. 3.2). This configuration is by far the least expensive, and it provides two full screens of information. The disadvantage is that the user has to look at two screens at once.

One Monitor Delivery with Video-in-a-Window

The signals from the computer and a video source can be combined on one monitor by installing an interface card in the computer (See fig. 3.3). This technique (often called video-in-a-window) passes the NTSC video signal through the card and displays it on a computer screen. Simultaneously, computer text and graphics can be displayed on the same screen. The video can originate from any NTSC analog source: camera, videodisc, videotape, or television.

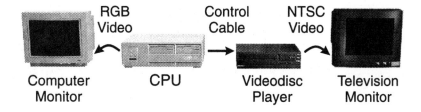

Fig. 3.2. Delivery with two monitors.

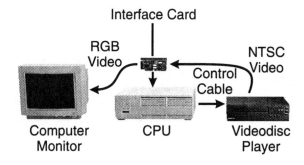

Fig. 3.3. Configuration for video-in-a-window.

Video-in-a-window technology has been used since the late 1980s. Popular interface cards include M-Motion by IBM, DVA-4000 by VideoLogic, and Super Video Windows by New Media Graphics. The advantages of using video-in-a-window technology include:

- A standard VGA monitor allows video input and computer overlays

- The video window can be resized or repositioned

- The hard drive is not affected because the video is not stored in the computer.

The disadvantages of video-in-a-window include:

- A "live" video source (usually a videodisc player) is required

- The interface cards cost several hundred dollars

- An interface card is required for delivery at each workstation

Overview of Digital Video

Video technology is undergoing a transition from analog video stored on videotape or videodisc to digital video stored on computer disks or CD-ROM. This transition is similar to the way music changed from analog audiotapes to digital compact discs in the 1980s. Analog video is continuous by nature; it can have any degree of brightness and an infinite number of shades and colors. Analog media is produced with electronic signals and always contains slight imperfections. These imperfections are noticeable as "snow" in pictures or "hiss" in sound, and they increase each time the material is duplicated. In contrast, digital systems use only a few discrete values that can be reproduced and transferred without errors. There are several advantages to storing video in digital form, but there are also some limitations. This section outlines the benefits and restrictions of digital video.

Advantages of Digital Video

Computer file format. Digital video is simply another computer file. It can be copied and reproduced without loss of quality.

Manipulation by computer. Digital formats can be manipulated easily and offer increased interactivity. With desktop video editing software, the images can be repositioned, resized, and recolored by a computer.

Networkable. Video in digital formats is easier to transmit over computer networks. Video teleconferencing over LANs and digital phone lines is possible with digital video.

One monitor. An additional advantage of digital formats (versus analog videodisc formats) is the hardware requirement. Interactive videodisc systems generally require two monitors—a video monitor that can display analog video and a computer monitor. With digital formats, the computer monitor can display both video images and computer graphics.

Disadvantages of Digital Video

Large file sizes. A major impediment to digital systems is that digital video requires an enormous amount of computer storage space. For example, when one videodisc frame is digitized, a file of roughly 3/4 megabyte is produced. Each minute of video represents 1,800 video frames, requiring over 1,000 MBs to store it in uncompressed form.

Requires high transfer rates. Another limitation of digital storage is the relatively slow data transfer rate of computer technology. It is very difficult for a computer to process digital video at the standard display rate of analog video, 30 frames per second.

Decreased quality. Because of the large file sizes and high transfer rates required for quality digital video, the majority of the digital video currently available has made compromises that produce images lower in quality than those on VHS tapes.

Digitizing Video

In order for video to be stored and manipulated by a computer, it must be converted into bits and bytes of computer information. This section provides an overview of the hardware and software necessary for the digitizing process.

Digitizing Hardware

Video digitizing cards are used to convert the electronic signals of the analog source into digital bits of information for each pixel, or part of the image, on the computer screen. Video digitizing cards make it possible to use a video camera, videotape, videodisc, or broadcast television as an input device and to display the video on a standard computer monitor (See fig. 3.4).

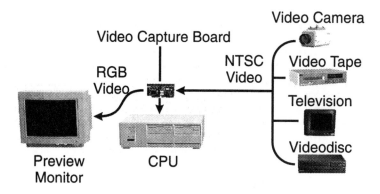

Fig. 3.4. Configuration for capturing digital video.

If the video is digitized and captured, it can be stored on a computer disk or compact disc. The analog source is no longer needed in the delivery configuration because the video can be displayed directly from the computer drive to the computer monitor.

Digitizing Software

The software used with the digitizing cards allows the user to select the frame rate, video window size, and color depth of the video image. All of these factors, which are set during the recording process, affect the quality of the digital video playback and the size of the video file.

Frame rate. The standard display rate for video on television, videotapes, and videodiscs is 30 frames per second. Because digital video files are so large, it is difficult for most personal computers to display the video files at the standard rate. In many cases, digital video producers will record video at less than 30 frames per second. At 25 frames per second, the difference in frame rate is not noticeable; however, many files are recorded at 10-15 frames per second and appear jerky.

Size of video window. Another method for decreasing the size of the video files is to decrease the size of the video window. In other words, if each video frame (uncompressed) represents almost one megabyte, a quarter-screen capture of the frame would be less than 250 K. Standard choices are full screen (640 x 480 pixels); quarter screen (320 x 240 pixels); and 1/16th screen (160 x 120 pixels).

Color depth. The number of colors in the display also affects the quality and size of the digital video files. The more colors, the better the quality, but the file size will be larger. The best resolution available is called "true color;" it is 24-bit and represents over 16 million colors. At 16-bit color, more than 65,000 colors are available, and 8-bit color provides 256 different colors. The impact of the color resolution is proportional—in other words, a 24-bit file is three times as large as an 8-bit file.

Compression Techniques

Compression techniques are used to reduce the size of computer files, including those that contain still and motion images. There are several general-purpose compression/decompression programs that can decrease file sizes, including *StuffIt* by Aladdin Systems, *DiskDoubler* by Symantec Corporation, and *PKZip* by PKWare Inc. These programs are used to compact computer programs and files for transfer or storage. For example, most of the files on the Internet are compressed by general-purpose programs, and many commercial software programs are distributed in compressed form because they require fewer diskettes. General-purpose compression programs are *lossless*. When a lossless file is decompressed, it will be the same size and contain the same information as the original file.

Lossless compression is not powerful enough for digital video compression because it reduces images at ratios of less than 4:1. To achieve the larger compression ratios needed for video, *lossy* compression schemes are generally applied. With lossy compression, some data are thrown away during compression, but the lossy algorithms are designed in such a way that it is difficult to see the loss because crucial information is maintained.

Video compression techniques employ combinations of within-frame and between-frame compression. *Within-frame compression* (or intraframe or spatial), discards redundant or extraneous information within each screen. For example, if a portion of the screen is all the same color (e.g., green grass), an algorithm will store the information once for the entire area, rather than storing the information for each pixel. Within-frame compression is sufficient for images that are displayed individually, but a more powerful technique is necessary with motion video for it to display 30 frames per second.

In *between-frame compression* (or interframe or temporal), redundant information is eliminated between screens. When the background of the scene remains unchanged for several frames, the computer saves the first frame in its entirety; then for the next few frames, it saves only the parts that change. Between-frame compression is used most for motion video because substantial redundancy exists between frames, and the compression ratio can be much higher.

Codecs

Compression algorithms produce encoded files that are much smaller than the original video files. To display the original image file, the encoded file is decompressed using a complementary algorithm. The combination of the two algorithms is called a *codec* (Compressor/DECompressor). Several codecs, such as JPEG, MPEG, Indeo, Cinepak, and Fractals, have been developed in the past few years. The codec chosen depends on the hardware, the desired resolution of the image, the storage space available on the computer, and the processing speed of the computer.

JPEG. The international standard created by the Joint Photographic Expert Group (JPEG) is a technique that uses within-frame compression for still images. The JPEG technique can generally reduce the file size at a 20:1 ratio without visual degradation. JPEG is excellent for individual images. A variation called *Motion-JPEG* can be used to compress each individual frame to create motion.

MPEG. The Moving Pictures Experts Group (MPEG) developed a non-proprietary standard for motion video compression. The MPEG standard uses between-frame encoding to eliminate redundancy between frames and within-frame coding to compact the information inside individual images. The amount of compression varies depending on the degree of redundancy in the video, but the compressed files can be reduced by up to a 200:1 ratio. A disadvantage of MPEG (and similar techniques that employ between-frame compression) is that most of the frames cannot be accessed individually.

There are three types of MPEG compression: MPEG-1, MPEG-2, and MPEG-3. MPEG-1 is the format used to record digital video for Video-CD, which is primarily targeted at linear movies that can be stored on CD-ROM. With this approach, up to 74 minutes of full-screen, full-motion video will fit on a compact disc. MPEG-1 is an open standard that any company can use without paying royalty fees. For example, CD-i and 3DO players have hardware options that provide the ability to play MPEG-1 movies. In addition, several of the video digitizing cards are including MPEG decoders for playback.

An MPEG-2 standard is being developed for production of broadcast video (equal to television quality). MPEG-2 requires a much higher data transfer rate than MPEG-1 and may be used for interactive television and other emerging technologies. MPEG-3 is being designed for High Definition Television (HDTV). MPEG-3 technology is not expected to be available for several years.

Indeo. The Indeo codec is a compression scheme developed by Intel as a software-only solution for displaying digital video. If Indeo is used in the software-only mode, it provides quarter-screen video at 15 frames per second on a 486 computer. If Indeo-supported hardware is installed in the computer, Indeo can provide full-screen, full-motion video on the same computer.

Cinepak. The Cinepak codec by SuperMac is one of the most popular software-only compression and decompression techniques for QuickTime. Compared to other codecs, Cinepak requires considerable compression time, but the resulting quality and compression ratios are excellent.

Fractals. Fractal compression is a powerful technique that is gaining acceptance. Fractal compression employs mathematics to analyze the similarities of repeating patterns of objects and images. Fractal techniques can offer extremely high compression ratios and the images are scalable, meaning they will adapt to the size of display monitor.

Fractal compression offers the advantages of fast decompression speeds, resolution independence, and much higher compression ratios than the other techniques. A recent educational application that uses fractal compression is the *Encarta* multimedia encyclopedia by Microsoft. Iterated Systems Inc. is a leader in fractal compression techniques.

Guidelines for Selecting a Video Digitizing Card

To record digital video, a video digitizing card or peripheral must be added to the hardware configuration. (See the resources at the end of this chapter for a list of digital video capture cards and digital video editors.) Recording digital video is very processor-intensive; therefore, a fast CPU is recommended. There are many factors to consider when purchasing a video digitizing card, including:

S-Video input. All of the digitizing cards can accept analog video (VHS quality) input, but some of the cards also accept S-Video. S-Video is used on S-VHS and Hi8 format video equipment, and it provides a better video signal.

On-the-fly compression. Most digitizing cards compress the video after it is captured and saved to the hard drive, requiring a great deal of hard drive space. A few digitizing cards can compress video at the same time as it is captured, saving space and reducing data transfer problems.

Multiple video inputs. Digitizing cards that can accept multiple video sources are advantageous if you want to digitize from several sources, such as a video camera, videotape player, and videodisc player.

Video output. Most of the cards can accept and digitize video, but cannot output the digital video to a videotape. Some of the more expensive digitizing cards offer this option.

Multiple formats for still-frame capture. Although most of the cards can capture still frames, a valuable feature is the ability to save the frames in a variety of common graphics formats.

Audio capture. In most cases, a separate audio card is required to capture the audio component of digitized movies. In the future, combination audio/video boards may become more common.

Video overlay. The ability to display the video in a window on the monitor without storing it on a computer is an important feature for previewing and editing the video.

MPEG encoder. Some of the latest video digitizer cards include MPEG encoders or decoders or both. These features enable the card to display full-screen, full-motion video using the MPEG compression technique.

Video editing software. Although video editing software can be purchased separately, often a combination package of hardware and software is available for a reduced cost.

TV tuning. A few video capture cards can accept television signals directly from television sets. These boards include a TV tuner on the cards.

Digital Video Technologies

Until recently, playing digital video on computers required special hardware. For example, Digital Video Interactive (DVI) required a special DVI-capable board for both capture and playback of the video. Two newer software technologies, QuickTime by Apple Computer and Video for Windows by Microsoft use software-only techniques to provide the ability to play digital video without additional hardware. This section contains an overview of several technologies used to record and play digital video, including DVI, QuickTime, Video for Windows, Compact Disc Interactive, 3DO, and HDTV.

Digital Video Interactive (DVI)

Digital Video Interactive (DVI) is a technique used to digitize and compress video, which can then be stored on a CD-ROM disc or hard drive. A proprietary computer board, developed by Intel Corporation and IBM, is used to decompress the video on a computer when it is played back. This technology allows over an hour of full-motion, full-screen video to be stored on a CD-ROM. DVI is an interactive medium and can store other digital information, such as audio, text, and graphics.

There are two formats used in DVI applications—PLV and RTV. PLV or Production Level Video provides maximum compression; the source material is prepared and sent to a mastering studio to have it compressed and placed on a CD-ROM disc. This procedure is quite expensive (about $250 per minute), but it provides the highest performance.

RTV stands for Real Time Video. In this format, the files are compressed on a personal computer that has an Intel/DVI digitizing board. RTV does not provide full-screen, full-motion video; instead, video compressed in this manner is usually one-quarter screen.

Advantages of DVI

Capacity. The capacity of DVI with PLV compression is over an hour of full-motion, full-screen video on a CD-ROM disc. If partial-screen motion is used, even more video can be stored.

Full-motion video. DVI was the first digital technology to display full-screen, full-motion video stored on a computer drive or compact disc.

Generic equipment. DVI hardware and software is available for MS-DOS and Apple Macintosh computers.

Disadvantages of DVI

Cost of hardware. DVI is hardware-dependent—the DVI computer boards must be installed in the development computers and all delivery computers.

Cost of compression. To achieve the PLV compression with DVI, the files must be sent to a mastering studio for compression. This procedure costs about $250 per minute.

Lack of standards. The compression techniques used for DVI are not currently compatible with the industry standard for MPEG.

QuickTime and Video for Windows

QuickTime (QT) is a format developed by Apple Computer Company to enable Macintosh computers to compress and play digitized video movies. Video for Windows (VFW) is a similar format developed by Microsoft for the Windows environment. A digitizing board is required to capture video for QT and VFW movies, but the movies can play back on computers without additional hardware. The only requirement for delivery of QT video clips is a file called "QuickTime Startup Document" in the system folder of a color-compatible Macintosh. Playback of VFW movies requires VFW software, the current version of Microsoft Windows.

Most QT and VFW movies currently play in a small window on the monitor (about one-quarter of the screen or less). Although the size can be expanded, the speed of the movies decreases substantially. In most cases, the movies play at about 15 frames per second, although the actual rate depends on the speed of the computer. For example, a QT movie on a Macintosh LC will play at a slower rate than the same movie on a Quadra or similar high-end Macintosh, and a VFW movie on a 386 computer will not be as fast as the same movie on a Pentium.

Advantages of QuickTime and Video For Windows

Do not require delivery hardware. The best feature is that no additional hardware is necessary for delivery.

Inexpensive. The file needed to run a QuickTime movie is distributed by Apple Computer with their system software. The VFW software is inexpensive and may be found on computer bulletin boards.

Synchronizes video and audio. When the digital movies are recorded, the audio and video can be recorded together; therefore, they can be synchronized.

Extends Macintosh interface for video. Because QT and VFW are recognized file formats, the movies can be cut and pasted between applications as easily as graphics and text.

Disadvantages of QuickTime and Video for Windows

Small pictures. QT and VFW currently support movies in a small window. As the technology matures, this size is likely to increase.

Requires large RAM. At least two megabytes of RAM are required for delivery of QT and VFW, and four to eight MB are recommended.

Requires large storage. Even though the video is compressed when it is stored, the file size is still enormous. A high-density diskette can hold only a few seconds of QT or VFW movies; therefore, most of the movies are distributed only on CD-ROM or large hard drives.

Less than 30-frames-per-second playback. Most QT and VFW movies display at about 15 frames per second, which results in a slightly choppy appearance.

Compact Disc Interactive (CD-i)

Compact Disc Interactive (CD-i) is a hardware and software technology developed by Philips and Sony and marketed by Philips. It was designed as a consumer-oriented interactive multimedia system, and it consists of a self-contained unit with a built-in processor and compact disc drive (See fig. 3.5). The video output from CD-i players can be displayed on a standard television set.

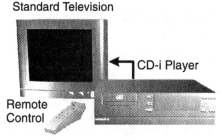

Fig. 3.5. Configuration for CD-i.

CD-i discs are created by producing a compact disc in a format that combines audio, video, graphics, and text. The initial CD-i discs were designed primarily for games and education, however, the technology is currently being implemented for training applications by several hundred companies.

Advantages of CD-i

Ease of use. The discs are self-booting. That means that all you have to do is put in the disc and turn on the player. There is no software to load and no commands to memorize; the interface is point-and-click.

MPEG-1 delivery. If an MPEG hardware decoder is purchased, CD-i systems can play Video-CDs with up to 74 minutes of full-screen, full-motion video.

Portable players. Small, portable players are very popular for business presentations and training applications.

Compatibility. CD-i systems can play CD-Audio and Photo-CD discs.

Disadvantages of CD-i

Lack of educational titles. The majority of the commericial titles focus on entertainment, although several titles for training are under development.

Incompatible with CD-ROM. Although CD-i can play CD-Audio and Photo-CDs, it is incompatible with CD-ROM.

3DO

Similar to CD-i, 3DO systems use an integrated player to output video directly to a home television set. These integrated players are a combination of a CD-ROM-type player and a built-in computer that has a very fast RISC

(Reduced Instruction Set Computer) processor. The players are designed for delivery only and are not compatible with CD-ROM applications. 3DO systems are targeted at the home and consumer markets; most applications are inexpensive and intended for entertainment.

Applications on 3DO discs offer graphics, sound, text, animation, and interactivity. 3DO systems can play audio CDs and Photo-CDs, but they are incompatible with CD-i and CD-ROM. Users interact with the units via a joystick or remote control unit. With optional hardware, the systems can also play Video-CD movies and provide over an hour of full-motion, full-screen video.

Advantages of 3DO

Speed for animations. 3DO players have extremely fast processors and can display high-quality animations.

Ease of use. The discs are self-booting. That means that all you have to do is put in the disc and turn on the player. There is no software to load and no commands to memorize.

Multiplayer capability. Numerous players can be linked for multiplayer actions.

MPEG-1 delivery. If an MPEG hardware decoder is purchased, 3DO systems can play Video-CDs with up to 74 minutes of full-screen, full-motion video.

Compatibility. 3DO systems can play CD-Audio and Photo-CD discs.

Disadvantages of 3DO

Compatibility. Although the players can play Audio-CDs and Photo CDs, they are incompatible with CD-ROM.

Lack of titles. This technology is very new, and there are currently very few titles. The majority of the titles focus on entertainment and games.

Expensive. Most of the applications for 3DO are games; however, it is considerably more expensive than competing CD game machines, such as Sega.

Video-CD

The software-only compression techniques (QuickTime and VFW) provide limited-quality playback of video files in a fraction of the screen. Video-CD (also known as White Book) is a new format that uses MPEG-1 video compression to provide a universal standard for high-quality digital video on compact discs. Video-CD is similar to CD-Audio in that it is designed as a linear format. In other words, you can select any track (or chapter) on the disc and instantly access a linear segment.

An MPEG decoder is required to play Video-CDs. This decoder is available in several different systems. For example, CD-i players will play Video-CDs if they contain the optional Full-Motion Video (FMV) adapter. 3DO systems can also be upgraded to play Video-CDs, and some of the new video digitizing boards include MPEG decoders. In addition, some existing audio CD players may be upgraded to play Video-CDs.

Advantages of Video-CD

Access. With video on a CD, there is no need to fast forward or rewind a videotape. The access is rapid, and most players can store a "program" of a desired sequence.

Worldwide TV broadcast standard. Different regions of the world use various standards for video. For example, the United States uses NTSC, Europe and Australia use PAL, and parts of France and Russia use SECAM. With videotapes, separate tapes must be recorded for each format. The Video-CDs are designed to work with all of the worldwide TV broadcast standards.

Storage. Video-CDs can store 74 minutes of motion video (more than twice the amount of videodiscs), and Video-CDs are less than half the size of videodiscs (4.72-inch diameters instead of 12-inch diameters).

Disadvantages of Video-CD

Hardware dependent. In order to play a Video-CD, an MPEG decoder must be present in the delivery hardware.

Maximum 74 minute playing time. Although 74 minutes may seem like plenty of playing time, most movies are over two hours in length, requiring two Video-CDs for delivery.

Limited interactivity. Video-CD is designed as a linear video format, with limited branching.

High Definition Television (HDTV)

The NTSC standard of 525 horizontal scan lines has been used by television and video since the 1940s. In 1980, the Japanese electronics companies proposed a new standard that would double the resolution to 1,050 lines using analog video. In the 1990s, the American companies responded with a similar standard that would use digital, rather than analog, technology. The advantage of the digital standard is that noise, or snow, on the screens would be eliminated. The disadvantage is that analog systems are much more efficient at transporting huge amounts of data than the digital systems.

For several years, it was a moot debate because the digital technologies were unable to transmit a signal capable of producing a television-like picture. Recently, with the advent of the video compression techniques, the digital plan became feasible, and won the approval of the Federal Communications Commission (FCC). Four American companies are now working together on the HDTV standard and expect to have equipment to implement it in the future.

Conclusion

Even though digital video is now feasible, videodisc technology is still a viable option for many multimedia applications. There are two primary reasons that videodiscs are still around: quality and capacity. Videodiscs provide display quality that is greater than that available on a VCR. On the other hand, the digital technologies provide a quality that is lower than a VCR. Videodiscs have a capacity for 30 or 60 minutes of full-screen, full-motion video on each side; digital technologies can only produce that capacity with expensive compression techniques such as DVI and Video-CD.

Part of the impetus for the trend toward digital video is that when video is digitized, it can be duplicated without any loss of quality. In addition, a computer can be used to modify and enhance the images. Many emerging technologies use video in digital form, and numerous applications are becoming available for trainers and educators. The chart in figure 3.6 provides a comparison and summary of several digital technologies presented in this chapter. As compression techniques improve and storage space increases, more and more of the video for instructional multimedia will be delivered in digital form.

	Manufacturer	Analog/Digital	Compression	Window Size	Media
Videodisc	Various	Analog	None	Full Screen	Videodisc
DVI	Intel/IBM	Digital	Hardware	Full Screen	CD-ROM Hard Drive
QuickTime	Apple	Digital	Software	1/4 Screen	CD-ROM Hard Drive
VFW	Microsoft	Digital	Software	1/4 Screen	CD-ROM Hard Drive
CD-i	Philips	Digital	Hardware	Full Screen	Compact Disc
3DO	3DO	Digital	Hardware	Full Screen	Compact Disc
Video-CD	Various	Digital	Hardware	Full Screen	Compact Disc

Fig. 3.6. Digital technologies comparison chart.

Videodisc Players

Panasonic Corp. of America, 50 Meadowland Parkway, Secaucus, NJ 07094, 800-524-0864

Pioneer Corporation, 600 East Crescent Avenue, Upper Saddle River, NJ 07458, 800-LASER-ON

Sony Electronics, Inc., 3 Paragon Drive, Montvale, NJ 07645, 800-472-SONY

Videodisc Production Houses

Call Optical Disc Corporation (800-350-3500) for a mastering bureau near you, or call one of the following companies:

3M Audio/Video Markets, Bldg 223-5 South, St. Paul, MN 55144-1000, 800-364-3577

Crawford Communications, 535 Plasamour Drive, Atlanta GA 30324, 800-831-8027

Laser Disc Recording Center, Inc., Cambridge, MA, 800-800-9864

Magno Sound & Video, 729 7th Avenue, New York NY 10019, 212-302-2505

Optimus, 161 E. Grand Avenue, Chicago IL 60611, 312-321-0880

Pioneer, 600 E. Crescent Avenue, Upper Saddle River, NJ 07458, 800-LASER-ON

The Post Group, 6335 Homewood Avenue, Hollywood CA 90028, 213-462-2300

The Post Group at the Disney/MGM Studio, Lake Buena Vista FL 32830, 407-560-5600

Telstar Editing, 29 W. 38th Street, New York NY, 212-730-1000

Digital Video Capture Cards

Advanced Digital Imaging (Digital Magic), 1250 North Lakeview Avenue, Anaheim, CA 92807, 714-779-7772

Alpha Systems Lab (MegaMotion), 2361 McGaw Avenue, Irvine, CA 92714, 714-252-0117

Calypso Micro Products Inc. (PC Vision Pro), 160-A Albright Way, Los Gatos, CA 95030, 408-379-9494

Cardinal Technologies (SNAPplus), 1827 Freedom Road, Lancaster, PA 17601, 717-293-3049

CEI (Video Clipper), 210A Twin Dolphin Drive, Redwood City, CA 94065, 415-591-6617

Computer Friends Inc. (ColorSnap PC PRO), 14250 N. W. Science Park Drive, Portland, OR 97229, 800-547-3303

Creative Labs (Video Blaster; Video Spigot Windows), 1523 Semoran Plaza, Stillwater, OK 74075, 800-998-LABS

Diamond Computer Systems Inc. (VideoStar), 1130 E. Arques Avenue, Sunnyvale, CA 94086, 408-736-2000

Digital Vision (ComputerEyes/RT), 270 Bridge Street, Dedham, MA 02026, 617-329-5400

Fast Forward Video (Bandit), 18200 West McDurmite, Irvine, CA 92714, 714-852-8404

Hauppauge Computer Works (Win/TV), 91 Cabot Court, Hauppauge, NY 11788, 516-434-1600

IBM (ActionMedia II, M-Motion), 4111 Northside Parkway, Atlanta, GA 30327, 800-426-2968

IEV International (ProMotion), 3855 South 500 West, Salt Lake City, UT 84115, 801-263-6042

Intel (Smart Video Recorder), P.O. Box 7641, Mt. Prospect, IL 60056, 800-548-4725

Intelligent Resources (Video Explorer), 3030 South Creek Lane, Arlington, IL 60005, 708-670-9388

JJ&K Enterprises (MR RAM GRAB), 5012 Whishett Avenue, Valley Village, CA 91607, 818-985-9407

Koala Acquisitions (MacVision), 16055 Caputo Drive, Unit H, Morgan Hill, CA 95037, 408-776-8181

Matrox Electronic Systems (Marvel), 1025 Stregis Boulevard, Dorval, Quebec, Canada H9P 2T4, 514-685-2630

Media Vision (Pro MovieStudio), 47300 Bayside Parkway, Fremont, CA 94538, 800-845-5870

Metheus (Video Zipper), 1600 N.W. Compton, Beavertown, OR 97006, 503-690-1550

New Media Graphics (Super Video Windows), 780 Boston Road, Billerica, MA 01821, 508-663-0666

New Video (Eye-Q), 1526 Cloverfield Boulevard, Santa Monica, CA 90404, 310-449-7000

Omnicomp Graphics (M&M Pro), 1734 West Sam Houston Parkway, Houston, TX 77043, 713-464-2990

Optibase (JPEG-2000; MPEG Lab Pro), 4006 Beltline Road, Dallas, TX 75244, 800-451-5101

Optivision (OptiVideo MPEG Encoder), 4009 Miranda Avenue, Palo Alto, CA 94304, 415-855-0200

Radius (VideoVision), 1710 Fortune Drive, San Jose, CA 95131, 800-452-5524

RasterOps (MediaTime), 2500 Walsh Avenue, Santa Clara, CA 95051, 800-729-2656

Sigma Designs (ReelMagic), 4650 Harding Parkway, Fremont, CA 94538, 510-770-0100

SuperMac (VideoSpigot), 215 Moffett Park Drive, Sunnyvale, CA 94089, 800-334-3005

Truevision (Bravado), 7340 Shadowland Street, Indianapolis, IN 46256, 317-841-0332

VIC Hi-Tech (VideoPacker), 2221 Rosecrans Avenue, El Segundo, CA 90245, 310-643-5193

VideoLogic (DVA-4000), 245 First Street, Suite 1403, Cambridge, MA 02142, 800-578-5644

Videomail (DigiTV), 568-4 Weddell Drive, Sunnyvale, CA 94089, 408-747-0223

Xing Technology (XingIt!), 1540 West Branch Street, Auroyal Grande, CA 93420, 800-294-6448

Digital Video Editors

Adobe (Premiere), 1585 Charleston Road, Mountain View, CA 94039, 800-833-6687

ATI (MediaMerge), 33 Commerce Valley Drive, Thornhill, Ontario L3T 7N6, 416-882-2600

Avid Technology (VideoShop), 1 Metropolitan Park, Tooksberry, MA 01876, 508-640-6789

IBM (Ultimedia Video IN), 11475 Reeck Road, Southgate, MI 48195, 800-342-6672

Neil Media (Video Graffiti), 2010 Stockbridge Avenue, Redwood City, CA 94061, 415-369-6345

VideoFusion (VideoFusion), 1722 Indian Wood Circle, Suite H, Maumee, OH 43537, 419-891-1090

Videomedia (Mac-Animator Pro), 175 Louis Road, Santa Fe, CA 95111, 408-227-9977

Digital Technologies

Other Compact Disc Technologies

3DO Company, 600 Galveston Drive, Redwood City, CA 94063, 415-261-3000

Apple Computer Inc. (QuickTime), 20525 Mariani Avenue, Cupertino, CA 95014, 408-996-1010

Eastman Kodak Company (Photo-CD), 343 State Street, Rochester, NY 14650, 800-242-2424

Intel Corporation (DVI), P.O. Box 7641, Mt. Prospect, IL 60056, 800-548-4725

Philips Consumer Electronics (CD-i), One Philips Drive, Knoxville, TN 37914, 615-521-4316

Microsoft Corporation (Video for Windows), One Microsoft Way, Redmond, WA 98052, 800-426-9400

Recommended Reading

Anson, L. F. 1993a. Image compression: Making multimedia publishing a reality. *CD-ROM Professional* 6(5): 16-29.

Anson, L. F. 1993b. Fractal image compression. *Byte* (October): 195-202.

Baron, D. 1992. MPEG-1 and MPEG-2: What's the difference? *Digital Media* 2(7): 20(2).

Barron, A. E., and Z. Boulware. 1993. Tools and techniques for repurposing videodiscs. *Educational Media International* 30(1): 9-13.

Barron, A. E., and H. Fisher. 1993. Affordable videodisc production: A model for success. *Tech Trends* 38(2): 15-21.

Beer, J. 1993. Video for Windows: Microsoft's latest multimedia winner. *CD-ROM Professional* 6(5): 44-46.

Blank, S.1992. Video image manipulation with QuickTime and VideoSpigot. *Advanced Imaging* 7(2): 53-55.

Brown, M. 1993. Video for Windows capture boards. *NewMedia* 3(1): 77-92.

Callender, J.1992. Videodisc players and recorders: Giving static presentations a new spin. *Presentation Products* 6(10): 42-44.

Doyle, B. 1994. Crunch time for digital video. *NewMedia* 4(3): 47-50.

Doyle, B. 1994. How codecs work. *NewMedia* 4(3): 52-55.

Drucker, D. L., and M. D. Murie. 1992. *QuickTime Handbook.* Carmel, IN: Hayden.

Epstein, S. 1994. Video on a PC. *Video systems* 20(2): 21-26.

Ford, R. 1993. New Macs put multimedia in the mainstream. *NewMedia* 3(12): 77-86.

Goldstein, J., and M. Wittenstein. 1993. Uses of interactive multimedia for advertising, marketing, and sales. *Multimedia Review* 4(2): 60-64.

Guglielmo, C. 1993. Lossy compression standards have extra squeeze appeal: JPEG, MPEG and related technologies maximize graphics compression. *MacWeek* 7(24): 30.

Gupta, S. 1993. Letting the computer drive computer video solutions. *Computer Design* 32(7): 77-80.

Hartigan, J. M. 1991. Videodisc: Something old, something new. *Video Systems* 17(7): 17-23.

Hecht, J. B. 1993. Using video: Basic terms and concepts—Part I. *ED-TECH Review* (Spring/Summer): 28-33.

Karraker, R. 1992. Computer-controllable laserdisc players. *NewMedia* 2(12): 39-40.

Luther, A. C. 1991. *Digital video in the PC environment*. New York: McGraw-Hill.

Nelson, L. J. 1994. The latest in compression hardware & software. *Advanced Imaging* 9(1): 56-60.

Nicolaisen, N. 1993. Sound and vision: Digital video hits the desktop. *Computer Shopper* 13(12): 614(5).

Reneaux, T. 1993. Videodiscs: A shrinking market. *NewMedia* 3(5): 44.

Rosenthal, S. 1994. MPEG's many advantages: The VHS of digital video. *Multimedia World* 1(4): 97-98.

———. 1993. QuickTime and AVI capture cards. *NewMedia Tool Guide* (November): 75-81.

Sirota, W. 1994. Interactive kiosks. *Multimedia World* 1(2): 72-78.

Stern, J. L., and R. A. Lettieri. 1994. *BMUG's quicker QuickTime,* 2d ed. Berkeley, CA: BMUG, Inc.

The videodisc compendium: 1993-1994 edition. 1992. St. Paul, MN: Emerging Technology Consultants.

Victor, T. 1994. Software video: Getting better all the time. *CD-ROM Today* 2(3): 34.

———. 1993. Don't throw away that VCR—yet. *CD-ROM Today* 1(1): 20-21.

Waring, B. 1994. Laserdisc players for multimedia. *NewMedia* 4(4): 37-38.

Wodaski, R. 1994. Microsoft's video for windows: A quiet revolution. *Multimedia World* 1(5): 83-84.

———. 1994. Secrets of video capture. *Multimedia World* 1(6): 89-90.

4

DIGITAL AUDIO TECHNOLOGIES

A Scenario

The instructional design team was excited about the new contract—over 20 hours of multimedia training to be developed for SONAR operators in the U.S. Navy. Audio would be an important element of the training because the SONAR operators were required to identify the audio signatures and specific sounds associated with different submarines. The operators also needed to be able to respond quickly and accurately to verbal commands from their supervisors.

First, the design team recommended the appropriate hardware, including digital audio cards, for the delivery workstations. Although an inexpensive card would be sufficient for the narration, a high-end audio card was necessary so that the SONAR sounds would be as realistic as possible. In addition to this recommendation, the design stipulated that the audio card be able to perform voice recognition, enabling the students to practice their verbal responses.

Following the hardware recommendations, the audio components were specified on the storyboards by the instructional designers. Next, John, a professional narrator, began recording the narration. The procedure was simple: he attached a microphone to the digital audio card, selected a sampling rate, clicked on "record," and read the narration. Each audio file was saved on the computer. John enjoyed the flexibility of digital audio; if he wasn't satisfied with the recording, he could always record again, rewriting the new file over the old one. He also liked the sound editor, which allowed him to view the sound wave, delete extraneous noise, and even cut and paste words.

After the digital audio files were recorded and the appropriate commands were written to play them from the authoring system, the final step was to add the voice recognition component. Although this technology was still limited, the digital audio card could be trained to recognize a series of discrete words. For example, an audio file would play the supervisor's question: "What's the heading of the target?" The student should then respond with the words "two-zero-two." The voice recognition technology converted the sounds to text and the authoring system judged the response and provided the appropriate feedback. Through the use of digital audio and voice recognition, the SONAR training was more realistic and resulted in better transfer to shipboard activities.

* * * *

Until recently, computers have been basically silent, except for an occasional beep or boing. Audiotapes, videotapes, and videodiscs provided the audio component of most training programs. Because of the decreased cost of audio hardware and increased availability of large storage devices, audio is now a major component of multimedia. This chapter includes:

- An outline of specifications for multimedia computers
- An introduction to sampling rates
- An overview of CD-Audio
- An overview of MIDI technology
- An overview of text-to-speech synthesis
- A description of voice recognition technology
- An overview of digitized audio
- Guidelines for selecting a digital audio card
- Training applications for digital audio

Introduction

Audio, in the form of voice, music, and miscellaneous sounds, is so common in life that many of us take it for granted. Audio is also an important, though often overlooked, component of multimedia. For example, it is very difficult to learn a foreign language without being able to hear it. Similarly, professionals in the medical field must be trained to recognize the sounds of ailing hearts. Although these sounds could be recorded with analog media, now they can be fully integrated into a multimedia program if they are recorded digitally and stored on a computer.

For many years, most computers did not have the capability to play quality, digital audio because the hardware and software capable of producing and amplifying the necessary sounds were too expensive or unavailable. Several factors have made realistic computer sound a feasible option. A multitude of inexpensive, high-quality recording devices for digital audio are now on the market or built into computers, and Microsoft Windows has enhanced the proliferation and ease-of-use of audio by standardizing the file format. A final factor in the increased use of digital audio is the availability of large storage devices (such as CD-ROM and large hard drives) at a reasonable price.

MPC (Multimedia Personal Computer)

Along with the trend to include more audio and other multimedia components into computer applications came the need to set some standards for delivery hardware. A few years ago, the MPC (Multimedia Personal Computer) standard was established by multimedia vendors to define a minimum hardware/software configuration for MS-DOS applications. In other words, if you have an MPC-compliant setup and you buy software marked with the MPC logo, it should work. After a couple of years, the MPC standard was enhanced, and an MPC-2 standard was set. The specifications are outlined in figure 4.1.

	MPC (Original)	MPC - 2
Computer	386	486
Hard Drive	30 MB	160 MB
RAM	2 MB	4 MB
Operating	MS Windows 3.1	MS Windows 3.1
CD-ROM	Single Speed (150 K/sec) Single-session	Double Speed (300 K/sec) Multi-session Photo-CD Capable CD-ROM XA-Ready
Audio Card	8 bit; 11kHz - 22kHz sampling	16 bit; 11kHz - 44 kHz sampling
Monitor	16-colors 640 x 480	65,536 colors 640 x 480
Interfaces	Joystick; MIDI	Joystick; MIDI
Peripherals	Mouse, Keyboard	Mouse, Keyboard

Fig. 4.1. MPC and MPC-2 specifications.

The MPC standards have helped to ensure compatibility among multimedia products. They have also affected the availability and configuration of several of the products related to the delivery of digital audio included in this chapter.

Sampling Rates

Bringing continuous, analog soundwaves into the digital domain of bits and bytes requires an analog-to-digital (A/D) converter. At small and discrete time intervals, the computer takes a "snapshot" of the level of the sound waveform and converts it into a number. This process is called *sampling*, and the number of samples taken each second is the *sampling rate*. To play the sound back, the computer reads the numbers and converts them back into soundwaves through a digital-to-analog (D/A) converter (See fig. 4.2).

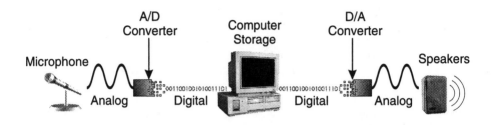

Fig. 4.2. Conversion process for audio.

The more times a sound is sampled every second, the more data there will be to recreate the sound, and the better and more realistic the playback will be. Most digital audio boards provide options to set the sampling rate between 4 kilohertz (kHz) and 48 kHz (between 4,000 and 48,000 samples per second). The sampling rate is directly related to the size of the digital file that is created. In other words, a sampling rate of 48 kHz will require 12 times more disk space than a recording at 4 kHz.

There are four main audio technologies used in multimedia: compact disc audio, MIDI, text-to-speech synthesis, and disk-based digital audio. Each of these four technologies processes the audio files differently and has a unique set of advantages and disadvantages.

Compact Disc Audio (CD-Audio)

Compact Disc Audio (CD-Audio) is the popular, consumer format, which can store up to 74 minutes of high-quality music on a compact disc. CD-Audio, or Red Book Audio, was first developed in 1982 (See chapter 2 for more information about CD-ROM standards). The standard sampling rate for CD-Audio is 44.1 kHz, providing very high quality sound.

CD-Audio discs can play in CD-ROM players, and they can be controlled through hypermedia and authoring systems by specifying the time code. For example, if you wanted to create a multimedia program that played a particular section of Beethoven's Fifth Symphony, you would specify the time code (in minutes, seconds, and frames) at which to start playing and the time code at which to stop playing. These parameters could be input into a hypermedia system or authoring program to control and play the audio (See chapter 8 for more information on hypermedia and authoring systems).

Many of the commercial CD-ROM programs discussed in chapter 2 contain some audio in the form of CD-Audio. These CD-ROMs are *mixed mode*—part of the CD-ROM disc stores the text, graphics, and video, and the other part stores the CD-Audio. For example, a multimedia encyclopedia with pictures of Beethoven and excerpts of his music stored in CD-Audio format would display the picture first, then the laser would travel to the audio part of the disc and play the music stored in CD-Audio format.

All recent CD-ROM players contain built-in digital-to-analog (D/A) converters that can play CD-Audio discs. When a CD-Audio disc is played in a CD-ROM player, the audio can be output directly from the CD-ROM player through speakers or headphones. If the computer contains a digital audio card, the CD-Audio can also be sent back through the audio card for playback. This approach simplifies the audio output by playing all of the audio through one set of speakers. (Note that the MPC standards specify that internal CD-ROM players provide an audio cable to send the CD-Audio through the audio card.)

Advantages of CD-Audio

Quality. CD-Audio is always recorded at 44.1 kHz, providing top-quality sound.

Durability. CD-Audio is recorded on very durable compact discs that are read with a laser. The discs do not wear out and are impervious to minor scratches.

Easy to access. The audio is stored by time code (minutes, seconds, and frames) on the discs. Most hypermedia and authoring programs can easily access the audio for interactive control.

Does not affect RAM or hard drive storage space. If CD-Audio is used to provide the audio components of a multimedia training application, it will not be affected by the amount of RAM in the delivery computer, and it will not require any hard disk storage space.

Disadvantages of CD-Audio

Read only. Audio stored on a compact disc cannot be changed or revised. This constraint can limit the flexibility of a program.

Limited to 74 minutes. The Red Book standard specifies that the audio must be recorded at 44.1 kHz. With current technology, this limits the amount of audio on each disc to 74 minutes.

Requires CD-ROM player. To play the CD-Audio in a multimedia program, a CD-ROM player must be connected to the delivery computer.

Musical Instrument Digital Interface (MIDI)

MIDI stands for Musical Instrument Digital Interface. The MIDI specification was established in 1983 to provide a means for a computer to communicate with a variety of electronic musical instruments and synthesizers. MIDI files do not contain digital samples of waveforms; instead, they contain instructions for playing specific notes, including the volume for the notes, the duration of the notes, and the instruments to emulate. MIDI technology provides a very efficient, compact method for storing and playing music. Although the ratio will vary depending on the complexity of the music, one minute of MIDI music can be 100 times smaller than one minute of the same music sampled as 44 kHz.

The configuration for recording MIDI music includes a computer, MIDI software, a MIDI interface, and one or more MIDI instruments. The instrument, such as a piano keyboard, can be used both to input the musical information to the computer software and to output the recorded songs. MIDI information can travel in only one direction on each cable, so separate cables must be used for "MIDI In" and "MIDI Out."

The instruments that play the MIDI files may look like real instruments (such as electronic keyboards), or they may be sound modules (devices that can generate the sounds of a variety of musical instruments such as bells, guitars, or drums). MIDI-compatible digital audio cards can also produce MIDI music (See fig. 4.3).

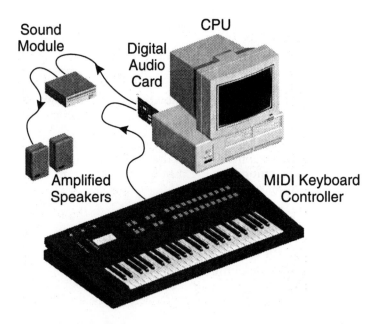

Fig. 4.3. Graphic of CPU, MIDI interface, keyboard, sound module, and speakers.

MIDI technology can produce up to 16 different channels of complex, sophisticated music. For example, it can play the sounds for stringed instruments, woodwinds, brass, and percussion simultaneously. Many kinds of extremely powerful and complex MIDI software programs are available. The programs range from pre-sequenced MIDI songs to extremely intricate composition software that allows you to score, edit, and print sheet music for your compositions. MIDI software also contains options to revise the music in relation to its rhythm, meter, tone, and many other parameters.

Advantages of MIDI

Small file size. MIDI files are a fraction of the size of digital audio files because the MIDI files store only the information *about* the sound, not the sounds themselves. Many computer games store the music in MIDI files rather than digital audio to conserve disk space.

Compatibility. The MIDI standard provides for the interchange of files between all MIDI synthesizers, sound modules, and sound cards.

Editing. MIDI software enables you to "edit an orchestra" by changing the parameters of the notes and the instruments.

Disadvantages of MIDI

Cannot create narration. Although MIDI technology is great for creating sound effects and music, it is useless for voices and narration.

Complex software. The MIDI editing software is quite complex. The composer must specify the length of each note and a wide variety of other parameters.

Unpredictable playback. MIDI files may sound very different when played back through different sound synthesizers and sound cards.

Musical talent is recommended. Creating or editing MIDI music requires a certain degree of musical talent. For those of us who are not musically proficient, MIDI files can be obtained via bulletin boards, the Internet, or CD-ROM collections.

Text-to-Speech Synthesis

Text-to-speech synthesis is another alternative for computerized audio. With text-to-speech synthesis, computer algorithms are used to translate printed text into spoken output. Text-to-speech technology is ideal for applications that require the computer to translate text into words, such as "talking" word processors and e-mail systems with audio output.

The highest quality and most expensive units for speech synthesis are found in business environments where they are used to read computer documents over telephone lines. For example, an employee might place a telephone call to an office computer to retrieve the latest e-mail. A text-to-speech synthesizer with the proper interface can read the documents to the employee. Many of the digital audio cards on the market include a text-to-speech synthesizer chip.

Advantages of Text-to-Speech Synthesis

Requires very little RAM or storage space. Because text-to-speech synthesis produces sounds using a set number of rules, very little computer memory is required.

Unlimited vocabulary. The potential vocabulary of text-to-speech synthesis is unlimited—any word (or group of letters) can be spoken by the synthesizer; the computer simply applies the phonetic rules to pronounce the word.

Disadvantages of Text-to-Speech Synthesis

Robotic sound. A major disadvantage of text-to-speech synthesis is the unnatural sound. Synthesizers do not have natural voice inflections, and the words sound very mechanical.

Phonetic pronunciations. Another limitation is that the pronunciations are strictly phonetic—the program cannot differentiate between words with the same spelling and different pronunciations such as "I like to *read*" and "I *read* the story yesterday."

Voice Recognition

The opposite of text-to-speech synthesis is voice recognition (also called speech recognition). Voice recognition gives computers the ability to perceive spoken words or phrases and to respond to them or transfer them to text. For example, you could dictate a memo to a computer and have your words converted to text, or you might verbally instruct the computer to change its display to 256 colors.

Voice recognition technology is advancing rapidly and is having a major impact on communications for physically and visually-challenged people and those who are nontypists. Voice recognition is also appropriate for numerous training applications. For example, with voice recognition, the verbal commands of air traffic controllers can be judged by a computer, and appropriate feedback can be provided. Voice recognition is also appropriate for simulations in environments such as airplane cockpits, where a keyboard would be unnatural.

There are two basic types of inputs for voice recognition systems: discrete and continuous speech. Discrete systems require the speaker to pause after each word; it recognizes only individual words. Most of the systems that run on personal computers are discrete word systems that can recognize between 120 and 30,000 words, depending on the software and hardware. Continuous speech systems can recognize word phrases; it is not necessary to pause while speaking. Although continuous speech is much more natural, these systems are also more expensive and require more sophisticated hardware and software.

Another distinction between voice recognition systems is whether they are speaker-dependent or speaker-independent. With speaker-dependent systems, you must train the system. In other words, the system displays words on the screen, and you pronounce the words until the system understands them. Although this training takes time, the speaker-dependent systems are very accurate and adapt much better to individual accents.

Speaker-independent systems do not require training and are more appropriate for general use.

Voice recognition is becoming much more accessible and affordable. The telephone companies have voice activated dialing, and many digital audio boards include voice recognition capabilities. Apple Computer now includes voice recognition technology (Plain Talk) with their A/V Macintosh computers, and the IBM Corporation has developed a Personal Dictation System (PDS) that can accept words at normal speech rates.

There are, however, some issues that remain to be solved before voice recognition can be fully implemented. For example, even after a system is trained, the error rate will increase if the microphone is placed in a slightly different position or if there is background noise. Emotions, scratchy throats, and articulation can also affect the recognition rate. It will be some time before voice recognition replaces the keyboard and other input devices.

Digitized Audio

Digitized audio refers to the process of recording sounds with a microphone or other input device, converting the sound into digital numbers with a computer, and storing the files on a computer drive. Digital audio recording with a computer offers the flexibility of recording and editing audio without the mastering process required by CD-Audio or the complicated sequencing required by MIDI. The digital files can be controlled by a variety of multimedia presentation and authoring programs, and they can be retrieved and played instantly. Digital audio offers inexpensive, accurate recording and manipulation of narration, music, and sound effects.

Digital audio provides many features for multimedia, but there are also some limitations and restrictions that must be considered. This section details both the advantages and the disadvantages of digital audio.

Advantages of Digitized Audio

Random access. Digital audio files can be retrieved and played instantly. In most systems, to access the audio, the user simply enters a "play" command followed by the name of the file.

Desktop editing. Editing audio files is very easy with software editing programs. Editing programs are often included in the price of a digital audio card or can be purchased separately.

Cost. Many moderate-cost, good-quality digital audio computer cards for MS-DOS computers are available. Newer Macintosh computers have built-in, high-quality audio record and play capabilities.

Disadvantages of Digitized Audio

Large storage requirements. Audio files require a tremendous amount of disk storage space. A stereo 16-bit audio file that was sampled at 44.1 kHz consumes over 10 megabytes for each minute of sound. If you are willing to settle for lower quality sound and record at 8-bits with 11 kHz, the file size can be reduced by about 90 percent.

Large RAM requirements. In many cases, audio files are recorded to RAM before they are saved on the computer drive. In this case, a large amount of RAM is essential, or the audio files will be limited to a few seconds each.

Lack of standardization in MS-DOS environment. The WAV format is standard for Microsoft Windows, but in the DOS environment, each sound card records and accesses digital audio files in a unique way. The best solution is to purchase an audio card compatible with the Sound Blaster card by Creative Labs, the only supported standard in this environment.

Lack of adequate speakers. To achieve adequate volume for the audio, additional external speakers are usually required.

Guidelines for Selecting a Digital Audio Card

To record or play digital audio with an MS-DOS computer, a digital audio card or peripheral must be added to the system. Recording digital audio is very processor-intensive, so a fast CPU, such as a 486 or Pentium, is recommended. You should also purchase speakers with built-in amplifiers, because the speakers on most audio cards are not very powerful. There are many factors to consider when purchasing a digital audio card, including:

Sampling Rate. The sampling rate is the number of times per second that the voltage level of the analog waveform is measured and recorded. Sampling rates are measured in kilohertz (kHz), with common rates including 8, 11, 22, 44, or 48 kHz. Some of the cards require that you select a specific rate from discrete options each time you record a file; other cards allow you to choose a sampling rate anywhere within a range, such as between 8 kHz and 44 kHz.

For the majority of training applications, a sampling rate between 8 kHz and 12 kHz is sufficient—it is roughly equivalent to telephone-quality audio. If storage space is at a premium, even 5 kHz will provide intelligible narration. For music programs, higher sampling rates are recommended to produce the higher quality sounds (22 kHz to 44 kHz). Even though you will not record all of your files with 44 kHz, it is best to purchase a card that can record at this level to satisfy the standard for MPC-2.

Bits of Resolution. The number of bits of resolution indicates the accuracy with which the digital sample is stored. With 8-bit resolution, there are 256 possible values; with 16-bit sound, there are 65,536 possible values, providing more exact measurement and playback of the sound. Although all 16-bit boards can play 16 bits of resolution, some of the boards are limited to 10-bit or 12-bit resolution for recording. The price difference between 8-bit and 16-bit cards is small; therefore, it is best to purchase the 16-bit version.

Compression Techniques. Some audio cards provide compression techniques that can reduce the file sizes by 4:1, 3:1, or 2:1. These techniques are lossy—some of the sound quality will be lost. Narration can generally withstand a degree of compression and remain intelligible, but music requires top-level dynamics and can suffer at even low compression ratios.

Disk vs. RAM Recording. If the audio files are recorded directly into RAM, you will be limited to very short audio segments (unless you have unusually large amounts of RAM). Many of the audio boards provide the option of recording to and playing directly from the disk drive. In this case, your file sizes are limited only by the amount of available storage space on your hard drive.

MIDI/Joystick Interface. The MPC (Multimedia Personal Computer) standard specification requires that sound boards provide external MIDI (Musical Instrument Digital Interface) ports to connect to MIDI devices such as a MIDI keyboard. Most vendors implement the external ports via a MIDI connector that plugs into a joystick port on the audio card.

Wavetable Synthesis. To play or create MIDI files, the sound board must have special hardware that can interpret the MIDI commands. In the past, the approach was to use a small FM (frequency modulation) synthesis chip on the audio card. An FM synthesizer approximates the audio waveforms of the different instruments; however, FM synthesized music usually sounds tinny.

Rather than FM synthesis, many of the current audio boards offer wavetable synthesis to record and play MIDI files. Wavetables store prerecorded samples of actual sounds and musical instruments and play back the notes according to the MIDI instructions. The results vary, depending on the number of instruments and voices stored on the card, but wavetable synthesis is noticeably better quality than FM synthesis.

DSP (Digital Signal Processor). Processing digital audio files is extremely microprocessor-intensive. A DSP is a separate processor that is built into some of the digital audio cards. DSP processors help the computer's CPU process the audio data. A separate DSP chip makes it possible to play audio while the computer is doing other things, such as displaying graphics. Another advantage of DSPs is that they are programmable—new features and standards can be included via simple software upgrades.

Inputs and Outputs. There are two basic types of inputs on digital audio cards: line level and microphone level. The line level input is used for input from a videotape or other recorded audio source. Microphone inputs will usually result in more noise and static than line-level input. Additional inputs may include interfaces for MIDI, joysticks, and CD-Audio. Outputs on audio cards can include headphones or speakers (See fig. 4.4 on page 76).

Compatibility. The standard file extension for digital audio files recorded and played under Microsoft Windows is WAV. Any Windows-compatible audio card will play and record files with this extension. Although compatibility is not an issue with Microsoft Windows, it may still be an issue with digital audio cards that run under DOS. Files recorded under DOS often have a variety of different, incompatible extensions.

CD-ROM Interface or SCSI Controller. Many audio cards include a port to connect a CD-ROM, so there is no need to have an additional controller board (and computer slot) for a CD-ROM. Some audio boards provide proprietary interfaces for specific CD-ROM players, but the better boards include SCSI or SCSI-2 controllers that will work with many different CD-ROM drives and other peripherals (See chapter 2 for more information about CD-ROM).

Voice Recognition. Some of the audio boards include hardware and software for voice recognition. These systems are usually speaker-independent with a discrete vocabulary of a few hundred words. Some of the

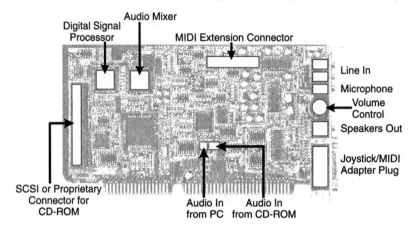

Fig. 4.4. Inputs and outputs on a digital audio card.

voice recognition programs have voice-activated macro programs. In other words, you can define a series of keystrokes and then record a word that will trigger the keystrokes. In this manner, saying "good-bye" could result in saving a file, closing a program, and quitting Windows.

Text-to-Speech Synthesis. Many of the digital audio cards include a speech synthesis component that can translate text into audio output. Speech synthesis usually sounds robotic, but it is a very efficient method for converting text into audio.

Drivers. A driver is a software program that comes with the audio card that enables the card to access the audio files. When you buy an audio card for Windows or MPC applications, it must have a Windows driver and it must be MPC-compatible. Microsoft Windows now provides drivers for most common audio boards.

Editing Software. Digitized sounds can be copied, cut, and pasted with sound editing software, just as text can be edited with a word processor. Many of the commercial audio boards provide sound editing software that display a graphic representation of the sound files (See fig. 4.5). Look for sound editing tools that include several levels of zoom so that it is possible to edit specific parts of the sound.

Mixer Software. Audio mixer software can be purchased with many audio boards or separately. This software enables you to control specific elements of the sound and mix various files, such as Audio-CD, MIDI, and WAV files, into one output file. Special effects, such as fades and inversions are often available in mixer software.

Audio peripherals are alternatives to digital audio cards for recording and playing digital audio. An audio card is not necessary for audio peripherals; the unit is attached to the computer's serial or parallel port. Audio peripherals are popular for laptop computers with few card slots, even though most of the audio peripherals provide only 8-bit audio without MIDI support.

Fig. 4.5. Sound editing software interface. (The horizontal dimension of the waveform represents time, the vertical represents volume.)

Digitizing Audio on an MS-DOS Computer

Most multimedia presentation, hypermedia, and authoring programs can easily incorporate digital audio files (See chapter 8 for more information on software programs). To digitize audio with an MS-DOS computer, follow this procedure:

1. Insert the audio card into a free slot of the computer.

2. Install the software program that controls the card (or use the Sound Manager in Microsoft Windows).

3. Plug a microphone or tape recorder into the audio input port on the audio card.

4. Select the appropriate sampling rate, bits of resolution, and so on.

5. Choose "record."

6. Speak into the microphone or play the tape.

7. Test the recording with the "play" command. If it is acceptable, save the file. If the file is saved in Windows, it will have a .WAV extension. If it is saved in DOS, the extension may vary depending on the card used.

Digitizing Audio with a Macintosh

The process for digitizing audio on a Macintosh computer is similar to the process on an MS-DOS computer—a software program is used to record and save the audio files. Macintosh computers, however, have built-in digital-to-analog converters, so no additional hardware is required to play audio files. Audio files recorded on one Macintosh computer can be played on any other Macintosh without adding an audio card or peripheral.

The newer Macintosh computers (LC and later versions) also have built-in recording capability. Most of the computers include 8-bit audio, and some of the later models, such as the Macintosh Centris 660AV and PowerPCs, incorporate 16-bit audio recording. If your computer does not have built-in sound, an external sound digitizer, such as the MacRecorder by MacroMedia, can be used.

Applications for Digital Audio

There are many applications for digital audio in business, industry, and education. The majority of commercial CD-ROM applications include an audio component and require a digital audio card (for MS-DOS computers). There are also many appropriate applications for developing digital audio in-house, such as custom interactive instruction, multimedia presentations, and audio notes in business applications.

Interactive instruction. Audio enhances instruction—especially for poor readers and students with poor vision. It also adds an element of excitement and provides auditory cues and transitions. Audio in multimedia instruction is also common because it reduces the amount of text required on the screen, freeing more space for complex simulations and graphics.

Multimedia presentations. Executives, administrators, teachers, and others are finding that their presentations are much more effective if they contain multimedia elements. Most of the presentation software programs, such as Harvard Graphics and PowerPoint, include options to quickly and easily incorporate audio files (See chapter 8 for more information on presentation software).

Business audio. Many of the word processors and spreadsheets that run under Windows or on Macintosh computers allow users to add audio notation by inserting a sound icon and speaking a few words into a microphone. These audio "post-its" are effective for explaining or annotating your work. Some of the audio notations will also transfer through a network with programs such as WordPerfect Office.

Conclusion

Random access to sounds, voice, and music is at the heart of multimedia instruction and presentations. Audio is expected to become even more fully integrated into the computer world in the future—some MS-DOS computer companies have indicated that they will begin building audio capabilities into the motherboards of computers; better compression techniques are under development; and the arrival of 3-D sound technology is imminent. The future should "sound" even better!

Digital Audio Hardware and Software

ACS Computers (Futura), 100 Sand Lucar Court, Sunnyvale, CA 94086, 800-282-5747

Ad Lib Multimedia (CrystalClear WaveTable), 350 Franquet Street, Ste. Foy, Quebec, Canada G1P 4P3, 418-656-8742

AITech (Audio Show), 47971 Fremont Boulevard, Fremont, CA 94538, 800-882-8184

Alpha Systems Lab (Cyber Audio Pro), 2361 McGaw Avenue, Irvine, CA 92714, 800-576-4275

Antex Electronics (Z1), 16100 South Figueroa Street, Gardena, CA 90248, 310-532-3092

Aztech Labs (Sound Galaxy), 46707 Fremont Boulevard, Fremont, CA 94538, 510-623-8988

Best Data Products (Soniq Sound), 21800 Nordhoff, Chatsworth, CA 91311, 818-773-9600

Cardinal Technologies (Digital Sound), 1827 Freedom Road, Lancaster, PA 17601, 717-293-3000

Creative Labs (Sound Blaster), 1901 McCarthy Boulevard, Milpitas, CA 95035, 800-998-5227

Diamond Computer (SonicSound), 1130 E. Arques Avenue, Sunnyvale, CA 94086, 408-736-2000

Digidesign Inc. (Sound Designer), 1360 Willow Road, Menlo Park, CA 94025, 415-688-0600

Digital Soup (Sound Professional), P.O. Box 1340, Brattleboro, VT 05302, 800-793-7356

Logitech Inc. (Sound Man), 6505 Kaiser Drive, Fremont, CA 94555, 800-231-7717

MacroMedia (DSP 16 Plus), 600 Townsend Street, San Francisco, CA 94103, 800-945-4051

Media Magic (DSP 16), 10300 Metric Boulevard, Austin, TX 78758, 800-624-8654

Media Vision Inc. (Pro Audio Spectrum), 3185 Laurel View Court, Fremont, CA 94538, 800-845-5870

Microsoft Corporation (Windows Sound System), One Microsoft Way, Redmond, WA 98052, 800-426-9400

Midisoft Corp. (Sound Impression), P.O. Box 1000, Bellevue, WA 98009, 800-776-6434

Multimedia PC Marketing Council, 1730 M Street NW # 707, Washington, DC 20036, 202-331-0494

OMNI Labs (Audio Master), 777 S. Street Road 7, Margate, FL 33068, 800-706-3342

Orchid Technology (Sound Wave 32), 45365 Northport Loop West, Fremont, CA 94538, 800-767-2443

Reveal Computer Products Inc. (SoundFX), 6045 Variel Avenue, Woodland Hills, CA 91367, 800-326-2222

Roland (RAP-10), 7200 Dominion Circle, Los Angeles, CA 90040, 213-685-5141

Sigma Design (Win Sound), 46501 Landing Parkway, Fremont, CA 94538, 800-845-8086

Sonic Foundry (Sound Forge), 100 S. Baldwin, Madison, WI 53703, 608-256-3133

Turtle Beach Systems (MultiSound), 1600 Pennsylvania Avenue, York, PA 17404, 800-645-5640

Voyetra Technologies (Audio View), 5 Odel Plaza, Yonkers, NY 10701, 800-233-9377

Wearnes Technology (Beethoven ADSP-16), 10105 E. Brokaw Road, Santa Fe, CA 95131, 408-456-8838

Recommended Reading

Barr, C. 1993. Sight and sound. *PC Magazine* 12 (October): 108(47).

Barron, A. E. 1992. Interacting with audio on the Macintosh. *Hypernexus, Journal of Hypermedia and Multimedia Studies* 2(4): 22-24.

Barron, A. E., and S. Varnadoe. 1992. Digital audio: A sound design element. *Instructional Delivery Systems* 6(1): 6-9.

Breen, C. 1993. Mac audio tools. *MacUser* 9(12): 193(2).

Burger, J. 1992. 8 steps to better speech recording. *NewMedia* 2(10): 74.

———. 1993. Sound thinking. *NewMedia* 3(7): 54-63.

Cron, M. 1992. Sound: The next frontier. *Technology & Learning* 12(5): 14-42.

DeVoney, C. 1993. Sound boards: Let Windows do the talking. *Windows Sources* 1(4): 382(41).

Grech, C. 1994. Pump up the volume: DSPs and wave-table synthesis make these cards sing. *PC Computing* 7 (March): 152(2).

Heid, J. 1993. Sound advice: How to add audio to your multimedia presentations. *MacWorld* 10(3): 118-23.

Kendall, R. 1993. Coming of age. *PC Magazine* 12 (April): 181(29).

Meisel, W. S. 1993. Talk to your computer. *Byte* 18(11): 113-20.

Miller, M. J. 1994. Conversations with my PC. *PC Magazine* 13(2): 79(2).

Millman, H. 1994. Finally, computers that listen. *Computer Pictures* 12(2): 15.

Murie, M. D. 1993. *Macintosh multi-media workshop*. Carmel, IN: Hayden Books.

Pickering, W. 1994. Computer: Take a memo. *Datamation* 40(1): 51(2).

Pogue, D. 1991. First steps in the sequence: How to get started in Mac MIDI music without really trying. *MacWorld* 8(6): 146-53.

Randall, N. 1993. AudioFile: More on the ABC's of sound cards. *CD-ROM Today* 1(2): 28-29.

Robinson, P. 1994. Speech recognition: Talking back to Windows. *NewMedia* 4(4): 74-75.

Rosebush, J. 1992. Sounds in CD-ROM—Integrating audio in multimedia products. *CD-ROM Professional* 5(1): 83-87.

Roth, C. 1993. 16-bit PC sound cards. *NewMedia* (November): 49-56.

Rubin, D. M. 1993. MIDI and multimedia: How to get started. *CD-ROM Today* 1(2): 40-46.

Samis, M. 1993. Wading through the confusing world of MS-DOS sound cards. *Electronic Learning* 12 (January): 30(4).

Scholz, C. 1994. Audio editors for multimedia production. *NewMedia* 4(2): 65-74.

Seymour, J. 1993. Making multimedia work. *PC Magazine* 12 (January): 99(2).

Sirota, W. 1994. MIDI sequencer: A buyers' guide. *Multimedia World* 1(5): 71-76.

———. 1994. Audio: A sound foundation. *Multimedia World* 1(7): 91-92.

Tully, T. 1994. TecKnow.babble. *NewMedia* 4(5): 102.

Tully, T., and D. Trubitt. 1994. The new wave of 16-bit sound cards comes to PCs. *NewMedia* 4(6): 67-80.

Wohl, A. D. 1994. Voice on desktop PCs: Recognizing the possibilities. *Beyond Computing* 3(3): 14-15.

5

LOCAL AREA NETWORKS

A Scenario

The meeting was unplanned, as are many of the meetings at the beginning of a new project. It all started when Adrianna imported an illustration that one of the graphic artists had just finished. While the image was what she expected, Adrianne noticed that the text captions were in a different font than the font she was using for the main text in her screens. Thinking that she might have the wrong font, she loaded one of Eric's screens for comparison. Eric was using the same font as she, but he had a different set of colors on his screen. It was obviously time for a quick meeting of the minds. If the group was to have any chance of getting this project out on time, they had better agree from the beginning on exactly which text and color templates they were using.

Adrianna opened the conferencing window on her computer monitor and selected the name of her group. Instantly, seven other people in the building had a flashing symbol on their monitors indicating that a conference was being requested. As each person selected the symbol, their work screens were temporarily replaced with the conferencing screen. After everyone had entered the conference, Adrianna selected clips of the illustration, her screen, and Eric's screen. These clips appeared on the other seven conference screens as well.

An active discussion took place through the microphones and speakers attached to each workstation, and several other clips were added to the workstation screens for comparison. Within five minutes, a short list was typed up and printed out on each group member's printer. It specified the text fonts, text sizes, and colors to be used on the screens of this project. Soon, everybody was back at work, confident that their individual components of the project would dovetail perfectly as the work neared completion.

* * * *

Such a scenario is well within the realm of possibility for a modern local area network (LAN) or wide area network (WAN). This chapter provides:

- An overview of LANs and WANs
- Basic components of LANs and WANs
- Details on peer-to-peer LANs
- Examples of network software
- Network implementation techniques
- Advantages and disadvantages of LANs
- Sources for additional information

Introduction

All of the activities described in the scenario can take place through computers connected in a local area network (LAN). Employees can use the programs on the LAN from any computer connected to it. With appropriate software, a LAN allows a group of instructional developers to work together on the same project. Messages can be posted so that groups of employees can read them, or a message can be sent to an individual employee's monitor. As illustrated in the scenario, technology now allows voice, images, and even video to be shared among those working through a LAN.

In a typical LAN configuration, one computer is designated as the file server. This computer contains a large hard disk drive that stores all of the programs used on the LAN, and it runs the software that makes the entire network run. Also, this computer, or a similar computer, may control one or more printers. If these printers are accessible by everyone using the LAN, the computer that runs the printers is called a printer server.

The other computers connected to this type of LAN are called workstations (See fig. 5.1). An employee working on one of these computers can use the programs on the hard drive of the file server as easily as programs stored on a drive in the employee's workstation.

A LAN makes it possible for all software to be centralized, so that a license can be purchased for each piece of software, providing use by a specified number of users. This simplifies the licensing issues that arise when many copies of a software program are distributed throughout an organization. A LAN is also able to automatically inventory all hardware attached to it, making it easy to keep track of the computer equipment. As outlined in the scenario, a LAN allows meetings to be conducted right from the workstations of development teams.

Many organizations use LANs for both the development and delivery of training materials. The development of training programs is enhanced by the connection of the design and production teams working on the training materials. Images, page templates, and lesson components can be transferred easily from workstation to workstation. The delivery of training is also improved, because employees can learn at their individual workstations, and

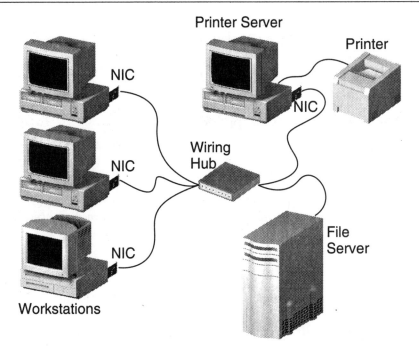

Fig. 5.1. Components of a LAN.

appropriate software on the LAN can monitor the progress of students through the training components.

Although the initial investment in a LAN can be high, the operation of a well-maintained, properly designed LAN will consistently cost less over time than would the operation of a group of individual computers. This cost reduction results from the centralization of software and management.

A simple example illustrates the relative efficiency of a LAN. Assume that 25 independent computers in a business have all been equipped with a popular database management program for storyboard development. Because the computers are not connected, the work of each employee exists only on the specific computer at his or her work space. A problem arises when two or more employees need to work on the same record. If copies of the database file are made for several workstations, it becomes very difficult to keep one single "latest" version. Changes to the database need to be entered separately into each of the individual computers.

Now consider what happens when a new version of the database management program and its documentation are purchased. Even though the instructions for installing the new software are clear, it takes 30 minutes to install the new software on each of the 25 computers. This is one of the most common problems with stand-alone computers—it takes a lot of time to properly maintain the software.

With a LAN and LAN versions of the database program, a different scenario unfolds. Because all software is stored on the file server, the database can be accessed by any properly authorized employee. The LAN software keeps track of who is working on the database and allows only one person to make changes in it at one time. That way, all changes are reflected in the single document. When the new version of the database program arrives, a manager or system operator spends half an hour loading the new software into the file server, and all of the workstations can use the new software!

LAN Components

A LAN is a collection of two or more computers, printers, and other devices interconnected in order to share resources. The components that go into a LAN can include cables, wiring hubs, interface cards, file servers, and workstations. Some of the more common components are discussed in this section.

LANs Connected by Cables

The cables that interconnect computers, printers, and other equipment are essential components of most LANs. A variety of cable types can be used, including twisted pairs, coaxial cable, and fiber optics.

Twisted Pairs

The least complex cabling system consists of simple unshielded twisted pairs (UTP) of wires, as are commonly found in telephone systems. If an office telephone system has spare twisted pairs, the telephone system and the computer LAN can be combined into the same bundle of cables by using adapters. A popular standard called 10BaseT uses pairs of unshielded wires, but the technical standards for the pairs of wires usually exceed the capabilities of the wire in older telephone systems. The 10BaseT system also uses centralized wiring hubs to create a star configuration (called a star topology) that allows easy connection and expansion of the LAN.

Simple UTP cabling systems are susceptible to interference. External devices such as elevator motors and vacuum cleaners can create enough electronic static to disrupt a LAN that operates on twisted-pair wires. Even ordinary telephone activity such as dialing or a ring signal in an adjacent pair of wires can create interference within a LAN.

Coaxial Cable

The next level of performance in LAN connections is provided through the use of coaxial cable (or coax). Although this type of cable exists in a variety of grades for different applications, it resembles television cable in form. In fact, it is sometimes possible to send several television channels through the cable being used to support a full-sized LAN. One of the most popular coax cables for networks is called *thinnet* because it is smaller than common television cable. This type of cable is also called 10Base2, and the thicker coax cable that resembles television cable is called 10Base5. In general, coax cable allows LAN workstations to be located farther apart than twisted pair cable. The thick coax cable allows greater distances than the thinner cable.

Rather than the wiring hubs common to twisted pair LANs, coax cables are often run in straight lines called bus lines, and workstations are connected directly to the bus line using adapters called taps (See fig. 5.2). While taps are easy to add to a bus line, a potential problem is that the bus line may be exposed and susceptible to accidental damage or disconnections. Most bus line systems are linear and do not have alternate paths to computers. As a result, a break in the line will prevent all of the computers beyond the break from having access to the network. Some coax systems incorporate a ring or star structure similar to those of the twisted pair systems to reduce the likelihood that the LAN will be shut down by accidental cable damage.

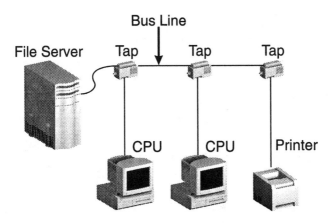

Fig. 5.2. LAN based on coaxial cable bus line.

Coaxial cable is almost immune to external interference, with the exception of direct lightning strikes. The cable is more expensive than twisted pair cable, and installation in an existing facility can be labor-intensive. Evolving standards for coaxial cable will soon allow very high data-transfer rates of up to 100 megabits per second (Mbps).

Fiber Optic Cable

A new type of cable being used in some LAN systems is fiber optic cable, which contains fine fibers of glass, instead of metallic wires, and conducts light, rather than electricity. Fiber optic cable offers many advantages over metallic cable. Extremely high-speed LANs are possible, with both audio and video capabilities integrated into the same cable. Also, fiber optic cable is immune to all forms of electrical interference because it is nonmetallic.

Unfortunately, fiber optic cable and the associated connectors are expensive, difficult to install, and difficult to modify. The last point is important. With twisted-pair or coaxial cable, it is easy to add additional computers as the LAN grows. With fiber optics, however, specialized techniques and equipment are required to make outlets for additional computers. As a result, hybrid systems are often created wherein fiber optic cables serve as trunk lines to link floors or buildings, and conventional metallic cables are used to connect the individual workstations to the trunk line. Fiber optic cables used in this manner often follow a standard called "Fiber Distributed Digital Interface" or FDDI. This standard allows data transmission speeds of 100 Mbps or greater. Figure 5.3 summarizes some of the basic characteristics of the various options for LAN cables.

	Wire Type	Typical Speed	Maximum Cable Length per Segment	Interference Susceptibility	Relative Cost
UTP	Twisted Pair	Varies	< 30 Meters	High	Low
10BaseT	Twisted Pair	10-16 Mbps	100 Meters	Medium	Low
10Base2	Thin Coax	10-16 Mbps	185 Meters	Low	Medium
10Base5	Thick Coax	10-16 Mbps	500 Meters	Low	High
FDDI	Glass Fiber	100 - 500 Mbps	2000 Meters	None	Very High

Fig. 5.3. Characteristics of LAN cables.

Wiring Hubs

The cables that connect the components of a LAN are often brought together in devices called wiring hubs (See figure 5.1 on page 85). A wiring hub can be a simple mechanical box that holds the necessary connectors (ports), or it can be an intelligent electronic device that continuously monitors and reports on the health of the cables and computers attached to it.

Wiring hubs often have specific names, such as the Multi Station Access Unit (MSAU) found in Token-Ring systems or the 10baseT Hub found in twisted pair Ethernet systems, but they serve the common function of providing convenient access points to the LAN. All that is needed to add another computer to a LAN is a spare port in the wiring hub and a cable with the proper connector.

Wiring hubs can range in price from under $200 to well over $1,000. A common mistake is to purchase hubs that provide only a few ports. While this may save some money at first, most LANs grow quickly. It can be much more economical to purchase a larger hub and have some spare ports to start with. Then, as the LAN grows, the ports will be immediately available. One 16-port wiring hub will cost less than two 8-port hubs. Also, because some wiring hubs use up ports to interconnect with each other, two 8 port hubs might have only 14 ports available for computers if one port in each hub is needed for the interconnection.

Wireless LANs

In cases where it would be very expensive to install LAN cables for a network, such as an old building that was not designed for such modifications, wireless LAN technologies might be an appropriate solution. A wireless LAN uses radio waves or infrared light beams to replace the wiring between workstations and file servers.

While wireless LAN technologies are still in a stage of rapid development, many popular systems are very user-friendly. In a typical system, such as Motorola's Altair Plus II wireless LAN, one component called a Control Module (CM) is connected directly to the file server. A second component, called a User Module (UM) is connected to a group of up to eight workstations. Multiple UMs are used in systems that have more than eight workstations or where workstations are spread far apart. Standard LAN interface boards are used in the server and all workstations. After the LAN software is installed, the wireless LAN based upon the Altair system operates as if it were connected with wires (See fig. 5.4).

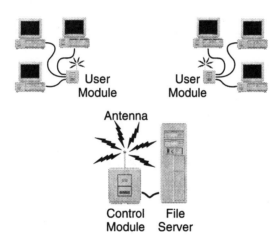

Fig. 5.4. Typical wireless LAN.

As with any technology, there are limits to wireless LANs. Most systems operate most effectively over short distances. The Altair system, for example, requires the server module to be within 130 feet of the most distant workstation module. Under less than ideal conditions, the maximum separation may drop to 40 feet. While wireless systems can be supplemented with additional equipment so they will work over greater distances, the cost of the system can go up dramatically, and the overall performance of the system might drop.

Network Interface Cards

A network interface card (NIC) is added to every computer in a LAN (See figure 5.1 on page 85). These cards affect the shape or topology of the LAN, the type of cable used, the data transmission protocol, and the data transfer speed. NICs vary in cost depending upon the type of system that they support and the transmission speed that they use, but they can easily add $100 to $500 to the price of a computer. Two common types of LANs are Ethernet and Token-Ring systems. The technical characteristics of these systems are complex, and the two systems are not directly compatible with each other. Techniques do exist, however, to interconnect or bridge individual LANs of different types together.

Data Transfer Rate

The data transfer rate of a LAN is specified in megabits per second (Mbps) and serves as a general indicator of the speed of a LAN. When a higher data transfer rate is available in a LAN, more workstations can be in use at once without noticeable delays.

As a general guideline, small LANs with fewer than 20 workstations that handle mainly e-mail and text files can function very well with data transfer rates in the area of 4Mbps. Larger LANs with 100 or more workstations or LANs that use sophisticated multimedia workstations require faster data transfer rates of 16 Mbps or higher.

File Servers

A file server is a key component of many LANs. It stores all the application programs and serves as the traffic director to keep all the computers and printers working together. Because the capabilities of the file server directly determine the usefulness of the LAN, there should be no compromising on the processing power and mass storage capabilities of the file server.

Processing Power

The file server is required to perform many operations quickly and, in some cases, concurrently. For example, at any one moment the file server might send a file to a workstation, route a letter from a workstation to a printer, and store an e-mail message for another individual. As a result, the file server must be a powerful computer. If it is an MS-DOS system, it should have at least an 80486 central processor, running at a 33 MHz processing speed. A Macintosh system should be a model that has at least a 68030 microprocessor.

Mass Storage

A large storage capacity is required for all the management and application programs on the network. Consequently, the hard drive storage space must be much larger than that found on an ordinary stand-alone computer. It is common to find hard drive storage in thousands of megabytes (gigabytes) on file servers. Most file servers also have ports available for additional hard drives as the network expands.

Because the primary purpose of a file server is to distribute files to workstations, the speed of the hard drives in the file server is important. If a file server with a powerful, high-speed central processing unit has a slow hard drive installed in it, overall performance will be poor. Experts insist on drives and drive controllers that are as fast as can be afforded.

The hard drives in a file server are among the weakest links in a LAN. If a hard drive fails, the results can be disastrous. Even if the data on a failed hard drive has been backed up on a regular basis, the LAN is useless until the hard drive is replaced and the files are restored. As a result, several technologies are being used to minimize the likelihood of a hard drive failure. One popular technique is called RAID (Redundant Arrays of Inexpensive Disks). This is a process of using two or more standard hard drives working together in a file server to provide levels of error recovery and fault tolerance. The hard drives in a RAID system work in duplicate pairs. If anything happens to one drive of a pair, the other drive (with identical files) takes over. This process allows a file server to keep working until the failed drive can be repaired.

Printer Servers

One of the economic savings of a LAN is the reduction in the number of printers needed. Stand-alone computers usually have a printer for each computer. This arrangement is not very efficient because some printers may not be used for long periods of time. A LAN allows one printer to be shared by several workstations.

When a printer on a LAN can be accessed from any of the workstations, it is connected to a computer that acts as a printer server. A printer server is a dedicated computer that is not used as a workstation. Because of the light computational load required of printer servers, they can be very basic computers. Like the file server, the printer server must be kept running when the LAN is in use.

A printer server runs special software that collects and stores files that are to be printed. As a printer finishes a job, the printer server sends the next file to the requested printer. When a printer server is running properly, employees will be able to continue with their work after sending a file to the printer, even if several other files are in line to be printed.

Workstations

Workstations are the most visible components of a LAN. A typical workstation is a standard microcomputer with a network interface card. This card is inserted into the computer and has cable connectors that can be accessed from the rear of the computer. Workstations do not need to have their own hard drives. Data or text files created by individuals can be saved on the file server, or they can be saved directly to floppy disks at the workstation.

Diskless Workstations

Some of the workstations in a typical LAN design may not have either hard or floppy drives. These diskless workstations can be used to operate programs on the file server. Any data that are created are stored on the file server, but there is no way for a user to enter information from a floppy disk or save information to it. Such a design greatly reduces the chance that a computer virus can be introduced into the LAN. Also, it is impossible for a user at a diskless workstation to make illegal copies of software or proprietary company files. Because of their secure nature, many LAN operators choose to set up diskless stations in locations that require LAN access but are difficult to monitor.

Multipurpose Workstations

In contrast to the diskless workstation, some workstations on a LAN have hard drives, tape backup devices, and multimedia peripherals such as digital sound boards and CD-ROM drives. In many cases, when an existing computer is added to a LAN, it is necessary to retain all of the stand-alone characteristics of that computer. For example, a graphic artist might want to connect his or her computer to a LAN to transfer images to co-workers, but he or she may still intend to use the video digitizer, the scanner, and the high resolution display as if on a stand-alone computer.

It is possible to set up a single computer to function part of the time as a LAN workstation and part of the time as a stand-alone computer. Care is required, however, to ensure that the LAN interface board and LAN workstation software do not interfere with existing applications. Such conflicts can be very subtle. In the preceding example, the graphic artist might find that everything appears to work fine after the LAN hookup has taken place, but later discover that the computer displays an "out of memory" message when a large true-color image is loaded into a paint program. The LAN workstation programs might have permanently taken up some of the computer memory, reducing the total amount of memory available for other functions.

Variations of LANs

Local area networks have been designed to meet a wide variety of applications. Because of these variations, it is difficult to define a *typical* LAN. For example, peer-to-peer, hybrid, and wide area networks have one or more characteristics that contradict the common definition of a LAN.

Peer-to-Peer LANs

Not all LANs use a dedicated file server. For example, A LAN might consist of a series of workstations where all of the CD-ROM drives and hard drives can be shared. Such a LAN is called a peer-to-peer LAN because all workstations are equal, and they can have access to the programs and files on other workstations (See fig. 5.5). While this approach does not require an expensive, dedicated file server, there are some limitations to consider.

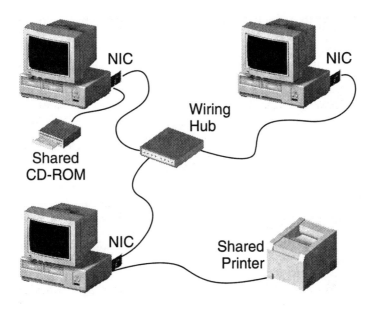

Fig. 5.5. Peer-to-peer LAN.

One constraint is that the LAN functions must be managed by the individual workstations. This means that performance on your workstation will be degraded when someone at another workstation uses your hard drive or CD-ROM drive. While this might be barely noticeable during a simple task like word processing, it might be completely disruptive while processing digitized sound or video.

Second, it is impossible to access files from a computer that is turned off. In a peer-to-peer system, all computers with shared files or peripherals must be running. This might be easy to accomplish in a computer lab, but it can be difficult in an office setting. For example, who has permission to unlock the vice president's office to turn on the computer when he or she is absent?

A peer-to-peer LAN is designed for small organizations, and it operates best when no more than 10 to 20 computers are involved. In addition, the users should have a reason to share files, as opposed to simply transferring files from one computer to another. If several people need to access and modify a single personnel database, then a peer-to-peer LAN might be a good choice. If all that is needed is to transfer text from one location to another, less expensive modem or serial port options may be more appropriate.

Another issue to consider is the expandability of the peer-to-peer LAN system. While some of these systems use proprietary interface cards and cabling, others use standard network interface cards and common network cabling. Although the peer-to-peer systems with standard equipment might be more expensive initially, they are easier and more cost-effective to upgrade to a file server-based network as needs increase.

Hybrid LANs

It is possible to create a LAN that uses two incompatible types of workstations. With proper interface cards, Apple Macintosh computers can be added to a LAN that has an MS-DOS file server and MS-DOS computers. Such configurations are not common because the Macintosh computers will not be able to run any of the MS-DOS software. At best, they may be able to store and run Macintosh-compatible programs through the file server and send e-mail and text files to the other workstations on the LAN.

Wide Area Networks

There are situations where workstations that need to be connected together are simply too far apart for a LAN. In these cases, related technologies are used to create a wide area network, or WAN. A WAN might connect several offices of the same company to one file server or allow employees to connect to the office LAN from home. In either case, telephone lines are used to tie the locations together.

Offices are connected by leasing special high-speed lines that allow such a high rate of data trasfer that the LAN functions as if all of the computers were in one building. Unfortunately, these leased lines can cost thousands of dollars a month if they are in constant, heavy use (See chapter 7 for more information on leased lines).

When an office LAN is used from a home computer, standard modems can be used to make the connections over normal dial-up telephone lines. Because common modems transfer data much more slowly than LAN connections, there are significant limitations to using a company LAN through a modem. For example, the process of loading and starting a word processing program stored on the company file server from home might take 10 or 15 minutes through a standard modem. The key to effective use is to install the large programs on the home computer, then use the WAN connection only to access small files such as business memos or individual database records.

A new application combines standard modem access to WANs with cellular telephone technology. This approach allows people with highly mobile jobs such as delivery personnel to use portable computers in their vehicles to update a central database as they make their deliveries. While wireless WANs are only now being perfected, many companies are already investing in the technologies that make them possible. It is likely that competitive industries that rely on mobility will soon depend upon similar technologies.

LAN Software

LAN software can be divided into three general categories: management software, application software, and groupware. Management software consists of the operating system and the software used to supplement the capabilities of the operating system. Application software includes programs used for productivity and instructional purposes. Groupware refers to software that provides communication between workstations.

LAN Management Software

Two types of management software are of interest to a manager who is considering purchasing or using a LAN for training applications: network operating software and workstation monitoring software. Each type has a specific and distinct function, and each can have a great impact on the usefulness and configuration of the LAN.

Network Operating Software

The file server uses a special network operating system (NOS) software to run the local area network. This software operates like a regular disk operating system, but it is able to keep track of many users at once. Complicated situations can arise when two or more workstations request the same programs or data files at the same time, and the network operating system must be refined enough to prevent mix-ups. For example, if one person is updating the telephone number of an employee while another person is requesting the telephone number for that same employee, the NOS must ensure that the second person gets the updated number.

The market for NOS software is becoming competitive, with most major microcomputer manufacturers and a number of major software publishers offering products. It is important to confirm that a selected NOS product is compatible with the network interface cards and application software on the LAN.

One of the more popular network operating systems is NetWare by Novell, Inc. The NetWare file server software is highly adaptable and capable of operating on a variety of network topologies using Ethernet, Token-Ring, and other network interface cards. Because NetWare has become one of the market leaders, many LAN application programs have been produced to be compatible with it.

Workstation Monitoring Software

It is important for a manager to be able to see, at a glance, what is happening on the LAN. Sometimes workstation monitoring software is part of the NOS, but it is usually a separately purchased enhancement. Appropriate monitoring software goes beyond informing a manager of the identity of the people who are signed onto the LAN workstations. Graphic illustrations of LAN capacity are common, and automatic alerts for questionable activities are often included. For example, most systems will alert a manager when multiple failed attempts to enter an employee password have occurred. This type of activity might indicate that someone is attempting to gain unauthorized access to the LAN.

NetWare Services Manager for Windows is Novell's network monitoring software. It is a graphical network management application that provides central monitoring, mapping, and control of network resources. It can display a map, with appropriate statistics, of the entire network and individual workstation activities. Many diagnostic procedures can be performed through this software, including tests of specific transmission errors.

Another type of workstation monitoring software is remote control programs like Carbon Copy for Windows by Microcom Software. This program allows an instructor at one workstation to observe and even operate a program that an employee is running at another workstation. This access to the employee's screen provides a direct method of training. This particular software can also work through telephone lines and modems. Remote control software is of particular value in companies where a centralized help desk has been established. A consultant at a help desk can use remote control software to help employees solve software problems by viewing the actual screens that are causing confusion.

LAN Applications Software

Most LAN applications software will be familiar to users. For example, word processors, spreadsheet programs, database managers, and many instructional programs will appear the same on a LAN as they do on a stand-alone computer. This is not to imply, however, that existing software can simply be copied onto the file server. There are two major considerations to keep in mind when evaluating the installation of existing software onto a LAN: software licensing and incompatibilities.

Software LAN licensing. Most software comes with a license that specifies the conditions under which the software may be used. If a software license does not clearly allow the use of that software on a LAN, the software should not be installed on a LAN. To do otherwise would make your organization vulnerable to legal action. A software license that does permit LAN installation will clearly specify how many LAN users are authorized to access the software simultaneously.

Software incompatibilities. Many single-user programs simply are not designed to work on a LAN. When such a program is installed on a LAN, unpredictable things can happen. For example, if two employees are using a single-user word processor through a LAN, they might discover that their text is being intermixed in one another's files.

Groupware

It is now possible to send and receive sound, images, and video through a high-speed LAN. In addition, file servers can access programs and data from CD-ROM drives and other mass storage devices. When all of the proper hardware and software are assembled, a LAN can be used to link the multimedia capabilities of several workstations in the manner described in the scenario at the beginning of this chapter. Software designed for this capability is called groupware.

Very few groupware programs have full multimedia capabilities at this point. E-mail and file sharing are by far the most common features, with group text conferencing close behind. Text conferencing, as in IBM's Person to Person software for OS/2, allows several people to interact with each other in real time by typing on their individual keyboards as they view a shared screen. The software keeps the text from each person separate. The screen might show a spreadsheet or image that is being reviewed. Small windows of motion video can also be created and shared using this software, but a standard conference telephone call may be required to share verbal conversation.

Other groupware systems, such as Lotus Notes by Lotus Development Corp., allow users to create "voice note" files that they send to each other. When such a file is opened by another person, it might display an image or spreadsheet while it plays a brief audio message.

Fully integrated sound and video conferencing also exist on workstations connected to LANs, but currently, such systems are at the high end of personal computers. For example, Silicon Graphics Inc. has a system called Indigo that integrates stereo sound and video into every workstation. Each workstation has a microphone and a small video camera to capture audio and video inputs. The software allows voice and live images to be transferred between computers on the LAN with a click of the mouse. Although this system is more expensive than standard PC or Mac computers, capabilities of the standard computers are increasing rapidly.

LAN Implementation

Selecting a LAN for a business requires careful planning. Complete details are too extensive to cover in this text, but this section outlines some of the most important points to consider.

Physical Resources

In an existing building, a major part of the cost of a new LAN is the wiring required and the labor needed to install it. If your business already has a usable form of wiring, such as spare telephone connections or pre-wired coaxial cable, then a major component might already be in place.

If your business has invested heavily in specific software, it is important to determine the costs of changing that software over to a version that is LAN-compatible. Sometimes existing software is compatible with LANs, sometimes it is not. If existing software is not compatible with a proposed LAN, then the cost of appropriate new software must be considered. Be alert for hidden costs. For example, if old database software is to be scrapped in favor of new, LAN-compatible database software, there might be considerable costs associated with the task of converting old database records to the new format.

Human Resources

It is most important to ensure that the LAN's strengths, which focus upon centralized control of resources, are compatible with the overall management philosophy within the business. If, for example, the administrative philosophy within the business is to decentralize resources and control, it might be a waste of time to try to implement a LAN.

A LAN is a major funding investment and frequently requires clearly defined commitments in human support. For a business LAN with 200 users, the basic activities of installing new software, deleting old software, and helping employees would require several hours each day. It is almost essential that one person be assigned the primary responsibility of operating the LAN.

Advantages and Disadvantages of LANs

There are a number of reasons why a business might decide to connect a group of workstations to form a LAN; however, a LAN may not be the best solution for every situation. This section discusses the benefits and limitations of LANs.

Advantages of LANs

Connectivity. LANs offer a great deal of efficiency through connectivity. All workstations on a LAN can share the hardware and software resources of the LAN.

Centralized management. In an office setting, groups can easily communicate and share information with each other. If the computers are used in an instructional lab setting, the LAN provides a centralized approach to monitoring the learning process. Appropriate software makes it possible to quickly evaluate the progress of any learner on the LAN.

Control of software against pirating. Because all applications software programs are stored and managed through the file server, LAN management software controls access to the software. It is even possible to install programs that are read-only.

Ease of updating or adding software. Software is easy to update or change because only one copy of each program exists on the file server.

Disadvantages of LANs

File server failure. Perhaps the greatest weakness in any LAN is that a failure in the file server will stop the whole system. It can be very frustrating to have a building full of computers that are useless because the necessary software is on a broken file server.

Cable damage. Problems with LAN cables can cause anything from minor interruptions to complete failures in LAN systems. Large, complex LANs might require complex diagnostic tools to help locate and correct cable problems.

Daily system management. One of the less obvious problems with LANs is that they demand consistent daily management. New employees must be registered before they can use the LAN. Software must be updated or added on a regular basis, and problems with printers must be corrected before unmanageable backlogs of print requests accumulate.

High initial installation cost. A LAN can be expensive to install. This is particularly true when a LAN is installed in an older building where the cabling requirements were not anticipated at the time the building was constructed. The apparent high price of a LAN can be misleading, though, because the actual cost of operating the same number of unconnected computers is usually even higher.

Conclusion

Local area networks are systems of computers, printers, and other peripherals that are linked together. Software is usually stored on one central computer, called a file server, and appropriate files are sent to the workstations as employees need them. Employees can send e-mail to each other through the LAN, and they can work together on group projects. Printers, CD-ROMs, and other peripherals can be shared by the workstations.

Local Area Network Resources

3-Com Corporation (Linkwatch), 5400 Bayfront Plaza, Santa Clara, CA 95052-8145, 800-638-3266

Apple Computer (Apple Talk), One Infinite Loop, Cupertino, CA 95014, 408-996-1010

Artisoft Inc. (LANtastic), 2202 N. Forbes Boulevard, Tucson, AZ 85745, 800-233-5564

AST Research Inc. (FieldNet), 16215 Alton Parkway, Irvine, CA 92718, 714-727-4141

AT&T Information Systems (LAN Manager), 7948 Baymeadows Way, Jacksonville, FL 32256, 800-247-1212

Brightwork Development (Sitelock), P.O. Box 8728, Red Bank, NJ 07701, 800-552-9876

CBIS, Inc. (Desk to Desk), 5875 Peachtree Industrial Boulevard, Norcross, GA 30092, 800-835-3375

Coactive Computing Corp. (Coactive Connector), 1301 Shoreway Road, #221, Belmont, CA 94002, 415-802-1080

Concord Communications Inc. (Trakker), 33 Boston Post Road West, Marlboro, MA 01752, 508-460-4646

David Systems (ExpressView), 615 Tasmin Drive, Sunnyvale, CA 94088, 408-541-6000

IBM Corporation (LAN Manager, Person to Person), Old Orchard Road, Armonk, NY 10504, 914-765-1900

Lotus Development Corp. (Lotus Notes), 400 Riverpark Drive, North Reading, MA 01864, 8003435414

Microcom Software Division (Carbon Copy Plus), 55 Federal Road, Danbury, CT 06810, 203-798-3800

Microsoft Corp. (Windows for Workgroups), One Microsoft Way, Redmond, WA 98052, 800-426-9400

Motorola (Altair Plus II), 50 E. Commerce Drive, Schaumburg, IL 60173, 800-233-0877

Novell Inc. (NetWare), Communications Department, 122 East 1700 South, Provo, UT 84606, 800-453-1267

Performance Technology Inc. (PowerLan), 800 Lincoln Center, 7800 IH-10 West, San Antonio, TX 78230, 800-327-8526

Phillips Publishing, Inc. (Local Area Networking Sourcebook), 1201 Seven Locks Road, Potomac, MD 20854, 800-777-5006

Robertson Caruso & Associates (LANLink Professional), 4514 Chamblee-Dunwoody Road #342, Atlanta, GA 30338, 404-512-0600

Silicon Graphics, Inc. (Indigo Indy), 2011 N. Shoreline Boulevard, Mountain View, CA 94043, 800-800-7441

Starlight Networks (StarWorks), 325 E. Middleview Road, Mountain View, CA, 415-967-2774

Ungermann-Bass Inc. (NetDirector), 3900 Freedom Circle, Santa Clara, CA 95054, 800-777-4526

Recommended Reading

Arnold, K. 1993. A buyers guide to desktop videoconferencing. *NewMedia* 3(11): 66-71.

Briere, D. 1993. No wires needed. *Network World* 10(42): 47.

Bruder, I. 1992. What's new in networks? *Electronic Learning* 12(2): 14.

Corrigan, P. H., and G. Aisling. 1989. *Building local area networks with Novell's NetWare.* Redwood City, CA: M&T Books.

Derfler, F. J., Jr. 1994. Peer pressure: peer to peer networks. *PC Magazine* 13(8): 237-74.

Gunnerson, G. 1993. Network operating systems: playing the odds. *PC Magazine* (October 26): 285-333.

Hazari, S. I. 1991. A LAN primer. *Computing Teacher* (November): 14-17.

Jensen, E. 1993. A few strings attached. *Network World* 10(42): 41.

Kinnaman, D. E. 1991. Networking: The missing piece? *Technology & Learning* 12(3): 28-38.

Lauriston, R. 1993. Serving up video. *NewMedia* 3(11): 52-56.

Lee, Y. 1993. Full wireless computing remains up in the air. *InfoWorld* 15(17): 1.

Marks, K. 1994. Cover your assets. (LAN Management). *LAN Magazine* 9(2): 139(5).

Molettiere, R. 1991. A guide to networking. *Media & Methods* 28(2): 40-43.

Palmer, M. J., and A. L. Rains. 1991. *Local area networking with NOVELL software*. Boston: Boyd and Fraser.

Stephenson, P. 1994. How does your network grow? (Network planning). *LAN Magazine* 9(1): 57(6).

———. 1994. Tilling the LAN. *LAN Magazine* 9(2): 83.

Strom, D. 1993. Novell broadens its horizons (Remote LAN access software). *Network World* 10(37): 1-14.

Taschek, J. 1994. Network the power of your best ally: Information. (CDROM drives on a LAN). *PCComputing* 7(1): 274(2).

Vernot, D. 1989. Get the whole story before you plug into a computer network. *Executive Educator* 11(3): 21-23.

Vandersluis, K. 1994. Expanding your AppleTalk net. *MacUser* 10(3): 133.

6

TELECOMMUNICATIONS

A Scenario

How can a person who is trapped by the weather at a radar base in Greenland prepare and submit a half-million dollar proposal that is due in Washington, D.C., in three days? That was the dilemma that Susan faced as she read the frantic e-mail note from her division vice president in Atlanta.

The sudden appearance of the request for proposal (RFP) was a surprise to everybody; it was one of those things that fell through the cracks of the Research Department. Unfortunately, the request was also made-to-order for Susan's team. For all practical purposes, the RFP required a carbon copy of the training that Susan's team was just finishing up. In fact, that's why she was stuck in Greenland. Several members of her team were out making spot checks for the summative evaluation of the training implementation. The Greenland site was one of the most remote but most critical, so Susan, the project manager, was selected to oversee the evaluation.

Now she had three days to get a full-blown proposal to Washington. If she could do it, the company had a good chance of being awarded a large project where most of the work was already completed. Susan started writing down her assets and her liabilities. First, she jotted down liabilities, as they seemed to be the most intimidating. Her list was short, but significant.

1. In charge of new RFP, but in Greenland.

2. Other key team member at a base in Australia.

3. All records of the current project are at the branch office in Orlando.

4. Travel, even if possible, would consume too much time.

Next, she made a list of her assets.

1. Several staff members at the office in Orlando know the project well.

2. All critical staff are available, even if scattered.

3. Washington branch office is located across the street from the agency that issued RFP.

4. All key players have workstations that access the Internet.

5. Main office and branch offices have a private wide area network (WAN) that connects their computers.

   Susan felt better. After a review of her assets, she realized that the liabilities were manageable. In fact, her team should be able to get the proposal together a day early. She would use the Internet to transfer the text of the original project proposal to Greenland and Australia where it could be edited for the new application. She had an ongoing e-mail "chat" with her team member in Australia and they had already discussed how to divide up the workload. After the edits were complete, her staff in Orlando would assemble the formal proposal and put it on the WAN for headquarters in Atlanta to review. Following headquarters' approval, the Washington branch office would use the WAN to finish the word processing and print the proposal. By the time it was printed, the cover pages with all of the required signatures would arrive by express mail and the package would be hand-delivered to the requesting agency.

   The staff around the world would be working some odd hours to get the job done, but that was nothing new. Susan saw from the Orlando menu on her screen that the text of the original proposal was ready for transfer through Internet, and with a few clicks of her trackball buttons, it was on its way to the hard drive of her laptop computer. As Susan listened to the wind howl outside the building, she realized that the next few hours of creative writing and editing would really be business as usual, even though she was at the "top" of the world and her co-editor was "down under" in Australia.

* * * *

Telecommunication techniques are not technologies that might become useful in the near future. They are here now, and they are used by millions of people every day. A number of telecommunication techniques are very important to business settings. This chapter examines those applications and explains the hardware and software that make them possible. This chapter includes:

-   An overview of telecommunications

-   Commercial online services

-   Business applications of the Internet

- A discussion of bulletin board systems
- Hardware and software considerations

Introduction

Telecommunications techniques are discussed in this chapter, and tele-conferencing techniques are covered in chapter 7. It is difficult to draw sharp lines of distinction between the two areas, but one distinction generally holds true—they use different treatments of time. In telecommunications, interactions do not usually take place in a real-time, conversational manner. More often, the communications take place over extended periods of time. For example, you might transmit a message to a colleague in Australia, and the answer might be sent back to you a day or two later. Some people call this "time-shifted" communication. It has the advantage that people who might not be available at the same moment in time can still communicate with each other. On the other hand, teleconferencing interactions take place in real time. You talk to someone and they respond immediately, as in a normal telephone conversation.

Telecommunications are supported by several types of systems, including home computers with modems, workstations on LANs, and large main-frame computers. For the computers to exchange information, they must be connected through either a telephone system or computer network system. There are three common activities that take place through telecommunication systems: electronic mail, remote access, and electronic file transfer.

Electronic mail (e-mail). E-mail stands for electronic mail, although a more accurate definition might be paperless mail. E-mail messages are created by a person on a computer workstation, transmitted to other computers, and read by one or more persons on their computer workstations. E-mail is useful only when a group of people have their desktop computers linked together through a mainframe, a LAN, or by modems. E-mail messages can be addressed to an individual, a group, or the members of an entire organization.

In many situations, electronic mail is more useful than traditional paper communications because it can be distributed instantly. An electronic memo about a problem might go through two or three rounds of discussion, and a solution found before a paper memo could have been duplicated and delivered to its destinations.

The use of e-mail can also reduce overall mail and telephone costs. Although the amount of savings depends upon the system, some e-mail programs make use of computer networks that are already in place and the added expenses of e-mail are minimal. Even international communications can be very economical.

Remote access. Many systems that can be accessed through telecommunications use files that are too large to transmit from place to place efficiently. For example, a database vendor might have many files available, each representing several megabytes. Remote access procedures allow you to command the power of the vendor's computer to run a program that searches for and retrieves only the information that you need. The specific information you seek, such as the author and title of a particular article, is then transmitted to your computer.

File transfers. Computer files often need to be moved from one computer to another. While the files could be copied to disk and sent via parcel post, there are more efficient electronic methods for transferring a file from one location to another. The exact procedures for electronic file transfers vary, but in most cases, a person can view a directory of files on a remote system, select those that are needed, and issue a command to have the files transmitted to the local workstation. The entire process is usually complete in a matter of minutes.

Commercial Online Services

Some companies use large mainframe computers to develop online telecommunications services that they provide to individuals on a subscription basis. The individual subscribers use home or office personal computers with modems or LAN connections to communicate with these online services. The expenses involved may include a registration fee, charges for long distance telephone access, and assessments for online connect time. The two main categories for commercial online services are database vendors and integrated services.

Database Vendors

Companies that produce online databases have historically provided them in print form to libraries or other large organizations. *Books in Print, Readers' Guide,* and *Dissertation Abstracts International* are all examples of databases that have been available in print for years. For the last decade or two, the publishers of such databases have used computers to prepare and update their databases. Database vendors such as DIALOG add powerful retrieval programs to make the information in the computerized databases available to consumers.

In general, the database publisher charges the vendor a royalty to make the database available to the public. The vendor charges its customers enough to cover the royalty and the cost of doing business. The database publisher gains additional income from the use of the database without having to create a whole new customer support structure; the vendor earns enough to make a profit; and the consumer is provided with a fast and efficient method for locating and using information.

The 1994 DIALOG catalog lists almost 400 separate databases from a wide variety of publishers. These databases include a huge range of titles from the physical sciences, social sciences, and the arts. With the uniform search structure supplied by the DIALOG organization, these databases can be searched one at a time or in groups. Results can be transmitted by modem directly to a home or office computer, or the results can be printed out at DIALOG headquarters and mailed to the customer.

Online database services can be expensive. The standard rates for databases in DIALOG range from $45 to more than $300 per hour of use. In addition, there is often an additional charge for each bibliographic record printed. Even when customers carefully prepare their searches prior to going online, a single search for information can often cost $10 to $20.

Most online database vendors market lower-cost packages to consumers in an effort to increase use of the services during off-hours, when business use is light. These evening and weekend packages usually limit the databases available, but the fees are also much lower.

Integrated Online Services

Integrated services provide a variety of services to consumers through home computer connections. Games, home shopping, e-mail, news, airplane reservations, information databases, and stock market quotes are some of the options available in a typical integrated services package. Several integrated online services companies exist, but *America Online* and *CompuServe* are probably the most competitive and well known. Both of these companies offer a variety of services, ranging from topical bulletin boards and e-mail to online travel reservations. Most integrated services providers place a strong emphasis on family and hobby resources. See the "Telecommunications Resources" list at the end of the chapter for additional companies.

The Internet

One rapidly growing telecommunications system, called the *Internet*, links computers around the world to provide international communication services. The Internet is a wide area network of networks, sometimes called the "global web" of information sources. It has roots in the U. S. Department of Defense Advanced Research Projects Agency network (ARPANET) that was started in 1969. In 1986, the National Science Foundation formed NSFNET, which replaced ARPANET and built the foundation of the Internet with high-speed, long-distance data lines. During the early 1990s, many networks connected with NSFNET and the concept of a global network became a reality (See figure 6.1 on page 108).

Probably the most significant factor in the rapid growth of the Internet was the definition of a single, common method of communication from computer to computer. All computers on the Internet follow a communication protocol called Transmission Control Protocol/Internet Protocol (TCP/IP). TCP/IP transmits information in packets, as is the case with almost all network systems. What sets TCP/IP apart, however, is that every packet of information has its unique international destination address embedded in it. The protocol allows each individual packet of a file to seek the best possible route to its destination. Depending on the routes chosen for the individual packets, they might arrive at their destination out of order, but information encoded into the packets allows the destination computer to reassemble the complete file into the proper order.

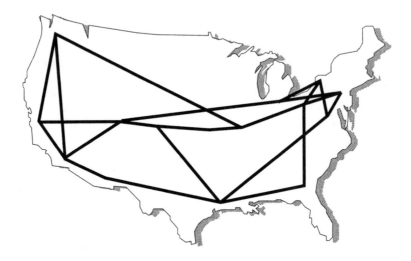

Fig. 6.1. Backbone of the Internet in the United States.

Because of Internet's roots in the Department of Defense and National Science Foundation, many government and university organizations provide Internet access to their employees. However, private companies and individuals are rapidly gaining access to the Internet. Companies can request their own Internet address or they can lease access through a vendor. Individuals often gain access to the Internet through commercial services vendors such as CompuServe, America Online, or Delphi.

Internet E-Mail

To send e-mail through the Internet, you must meet some very basic requirements. First, you must have access to a host computer on the Internet. This access might be through a mainframe or minicomputer at a university or business, or it might be through a commercial service vendor.

Second, you need an account that provides an Internet user address. Such an address might be something like orwig@pegasus.cc.ucf.edu. The address is made up of two components. To the left of the @ symbol is the identification, or user name. In this example, orwig is the user name for Gary Orwig. To the right of the @ symbol is the Internet designation of the user's system, called the host name, or domain name. The host name follows a predefined structure. The last right-hand component (edu) represents a type of organization. Some common types are "edu" for educational, "com" for commercial, and "mil" for military. Sometimes a country indicator (e.g., "uk" for United Kingdom) is placed in this position (See fig. 6.2). The remainder of the host name identifies a specific computer. In this example, pegasus.cc.ucf identifies the computer called "Pegasus" at the Computer Center (cc) of the University of Central Florida (ucf)

Major Domains	
EDU	Education
COM	Commercial Organization
MIL	Military
GOV	Government Sites
NET	Special Network Resources
ORG	Other Organizations
UK	United Kingdom
CA	Canada

Fig. 6.2. Types of organizations and their Internet identifiers.

Finally, you need a program that makes it easy to use the Internet e-mail. PINE, by the University of Washington, is one of the most popular programs is called PINE. PINE runs on the host computer and provides menus that allow users to make simple choices for reading messages, composing and sending messages, and creating address lists.

With these components (a host computer, an Internet user address, and a software interface), it is a simple matter to use an office desktop computer, a LAN computer, or a home computer to compose, send, and receive e-mail on a global scale.

Internet Remote Access

E-mail provides an avenue for person-to-person communication, but much of the database information in the world exists in various forms such as online library catalogs, periodical indexes, stored weather satellite images, and listings of public domain software. A major benefit of the Internet is the ability to connect your computer directly to another computer system at a remote location. The remote access feature of the Internet provides fast, easy entry into huge storehouses of information. Most of the information sources can be accessed without charge, but some commercial activities such as the information database vendor DIALOG or the Official Airline Guide charge a fee.

The Internet method of accessing these databases is through a program called telnet. When the command "telnet spacelink.msfc.nasa.gov" is issued from a computer connected to the Internet, that computer connects to the NASA computer in Alabama. This computer is open to the public—just log in as "guest." After you have logged in, you can use the NASA computer to search the directories, download images and programs, and conduct research in the files. There are thousands of telnet sites around the world that allow anyone with Internet access to use their resources.

Internet File Transfers

The third major component of Internet allows individuals to transfer files from a computer at one location to a computer at another. The files that are transferred might be text, databases, spreadsheets, public domain programs, images of X-rays, music, or anything else that can be digitized into a computer format. The process of transferring a program file on the Internet is FTP, which stands for file transfer protocol. The specific procedures for using FTP are too detailed for this text, however, a typical transfer might proceed as follows:

> You have just loaded a new version of your operating system into your computer. After you reboot the computer, you discover that your audio card no longer plays audio properly. After looking through the manuals, you determine that you need an updated device driver. (A device driver is a small program that links the audio card to the operating system.)
>
> The problem is that the audio card was made in Japan, and there doesn't seem to be a domestic source for technical support. The manual does, however, give an Internet address for the Japanese technical support office, so you can send an e-mail message to the address and explain the problem. It is obvious that someone in Japan understands your problem, because the next day you have an e-mail message that provides specific details on how to use FTP to download the new driver that you need. You simply need to log on to your Internet account, type the appropriate FTP and "get" commands, and within minutes you can transfer and download the correct software driver program.

It might seem like there are fairly limited uses to the FTP process, but when you become aware of the incredible number of images (weather satellite pictures, NASA launches, museum pieces), sound files (music, sound effects, MIDI files), and public domain software programs available, the issue quickly becomes one of limiting use rather than limited use. A person could spend hours a day for months downloading public access files and still not touch the bottom of the bucket!

Internet Help

The Internet is huge and can easily overwhelm the unfamiliar user. Many resources are now available to help users accomplish their goals on the Internet. A variety of programs on the Internet assist users in locating and accessing files and resources. Many of these Internet help tools have catchy names like Gopher, Archie, and Mosiac. Archie is a program that searches the

Internet for files that are available to be transferred. You do not have to know the exact name or location of the file, because Archie will use descriptions that you type in to search out and report all likely files and locations back to you.

Gopher programs present you with menus of the information available on the Internet. When you make a selection, the Gopher program will automatically "go for" the requested information, so you do not need to know the specific address or log in procedure to get what you want. Newer programs such as Mosaic create multimedia links to the Internet. These programs function in much the same way as the Gopher programs, but images are automatically displayed and sounds are played as they arrive. However, advanced programs like Mosaic require high-speed connections into the Internet that might not be available to home users.

There is a growing number of books and online help programs to teach you how to use the Internet. Some are very basic and will get you started; others address the more complex aspects of Internet.

Bulletin Board Systems

If you are not associated with an institution with an Internet node, but you still need electronic communications among your employees, you might consider an electronic bulletin board system (BBS). A BBS can operate on a basic personal computer with a telephone line, modem, and the appropriate software. Operating on a much smaller scale than the Internet, a BBS can still provide several basic services, such as e-mail, conferencing, and file transfers.

E-Mail on Bulletin Board Systems

Many BBSs are set up primarily to serve as an e-mail service for a specific group of people. Clubs, professional organizations, businesses, and offices often use the e-mail function of a BBS more heavily than any other feature. For example, if a BBS is running 24 hours a day at your business, employees can use their modems at night to check for messages, contact customers, or call in sick. In some cases, a BBS can also serve as an Internet e-mail connection for its users.

Bulletin Board Conferencing

Bulletin board conferencing is somewhat like e-mail, but the messages are addressed to groups rather than individuals. Anyone who registers to the conference will be able to read and respond to the conference message. For example, an office bulletin board system might have a variety of conferences, including one for employees who travel frequently. Any employee who is registered on the system and interested in travel will be able to read and respond to messages on that conference. Conferencing is a way to break up a large system into smaller components that relate to specific topics.

File Transfers on Bulletin Boards

Almost any BBS can be set up to transfer files. This application is both one of the most useful and one of the most troublesome of all bulletin board features. When used properly, it functions much like the FTP process in Internet. Many companies distribute software updates to their customers through BBSs. But when used improperly, BBS file transfers allow individuals to pirate copyrighted software or to introduce and distribute computer viruses. It is possible to set up a BBS that allows only limited file transfers and to maintain reasonable control over the process.

Telecommunications—Methods of Access

Telecommunications can involve a variety of computers including mainframe computers, local area networks, and home or office computers connected by modems. For example, a message may travel from a home computer with a modem in Tampa to a mainframe computer in Tallahassee, through the Internet to a mainframe in Germany, and finally to a workstation on a local area network in Hanover. This section presents some of the basics about the hardware and platforms necessary for telecommunications in business settings.

Mainframe Computers

The earliest telecommunications systems were based on mainframe computers and other powerful computers in universities and other organizations. Workstations connected to these systems can be used to transfer files, send messages, and access remote information.

It is now a common practice to link home computers to company mainframes through modems or digital telephone lines. Some businesses are experimenting with work-at-home plans in which employees are encouraged to spend several days a week doing their regular work at home, with mainframe computer services provided through telephone lines and modems. Employees use home personal computers to do much of their work and link into the mainframe when additional data or greater processing power is required.

Local and Wide Area Networks

Local area networks (LANs) and wide area networks (WANs) are discussed in detail in chapter 5, but it is appropriate to mention here that almost any LAN or WAN can provide e-mail, file transfer, and remote access features. Some LAN systems integrate an e-mail system into the basic software package, but LAN operators usually purchase a separate add-on package such as *WordPerfect Office*.

A LAN or WAN can also be linked to home computers through modems. This connection allows the home computer to access files, send e-mail, and execute programs that are on the LAN computers. With the appropriate connecting software, it is possible to "take over" the keyboard of an office computer on a LAN from another location in the office or at home. The programs run on the office computer, but their results are sent to the video display of the distant computer. License agreements of many software applications prohibit the sending of the actual program to remote sites. While the remote access process through a LAN or WAN is slower than normal processing, it does allow individuals to run programs from a distance without violating license restrictions.

Modems

In most cases, LANs, WANs, and mainframes are connected to each other through digital data lines. Office workstations and home computers often link into these systems through regular telephone lines. Most standard telephone lines transmit only audio tones, like human voices. A computer, on the other hand, manipulates digital information in a binary code of 0s and 1s. The modem translates (or modulates) the 0s and 1s of an outgoing computer message into a fluctuating tone that travels through the telephone line. As this tone comes through the telephone line at a distant site, another modem translates (or demodulates) it back into the 0s and 1s of the binary language of a computer. Thus, the MO (Modulator) DEM (DEModulator) allows the two computers to behave as though they are connected directly together, even though they might be thousands of miles apart (See fig. 6.3).

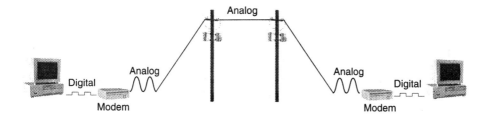

Fig. 6.3. Using a modem for telecommunications.

Modem Speed

Over the last 10 years, manufacturers have been able to increase the transfer rate or speed of modems significantly. While this improvement has been due in part to improvements in telephone lines, the largest improvements have come from discoveries in how to send and receive more information over the telephone lines and how to compensate for common telephone line interference.

The modern measurement of the speed of modems, bits per second (bps), has replaced an earlier term (baud). A bit is a binary digit, having a value of 0 or 1. The more bits a modem can process per second, the faster it can send and receive data. It takes several bits to define each character and several more to separate the characters, meaning that it takes about 10 bits to transmit or receive a single character of information. A 2,400 bps modem can transmit or receive about 240 characters per second. This sentence, which is 103 characters long (counting spaces), would require about 0.4 seconds to transmit. At 9,600 bps, the same sentence would take about 0.1 second.

Until recently, a modem that operated at 2,400 bps was considered fast. Now 2,400 bps modems are considered outdated, and 9,600 bps or faster modems dominate new sales. By the time this book is in print, modems that transmit at 28,800 bps will be readily available. Faster modems mean less time connected to a telephone. Shorter telephone connection times result in lower charges for long-distance calls and lower connection fees for many services that charge a single rate by the hour.

Internal and External Modems

Modems can either be installed inside the computer, or they can sit next to the computer in their own box. There are advantages to each type of modem. The advantages of one type of modem generally turn out to be the disadvantages of the other type. Internal modems are preferred for portable or laptop computers because they become part of the computer and cannot be left behind. External modems can be moved from one computer to another with ease and make use of a communications port that is standard on most microcomputers.

Modem Software

Modems allow computers to communicate through standard telephone lines, but the computers still have a lot of work to do. Telecommunications software are the computer programs that operate modems. These programs perform a number of activities. For example, a telecommunications software program would format arriving text for your computer screen by inserting carriage returns and line feeds where necessary. They may also contain a dialing directory, so that you can select the appropriate number from a list. Once selected, the telephone number is dialed and the modem settings associated with that telephone number are used to prepare the modem for action.

There are many commercial software programs for telecommunications now available. Some programs, such as Procomm 2.4 for MS-DOS computers, were originally distributed as shareware. This particular program has been very popular in office systems, because it can be distributed freely in its original form. The current versions of Procomm for both MS-DOS and Windows systems are sold on the regular retail market. Although Procomm Plus for Windows is more expensive than the original shareware version, its added features are well worth the additional cost. A variety of telecommunications programs such as White Knight, Z-Term (shareware), and Microphone Pro are available for Macintosh computers.

Fax Modems

Facsimile machines, or fax machines as they are frequently called, have become almost as common as modems. Fax machines are used to send copies of paper documents from one location to another. The machines function in much the same way as modems in that they generate tones that are sent over standard telephone lines.

It is now possible to purchase modems that can also send and receive fax messages. Such a modem still allows one computer to connect to another to share data, but it can also connect to a distant fax machine. When it operates as a fax machine, it can receive an image of whatever the fax machine at the other end is sending. With proper software, this image can be printed, stored, or immediately displayed on the computer screen. The image might contain text, numbers, line drawings, or photographs; however, it is only an image. Even if the fax is entirely text, the text cannot be fed directly into a word processor for editing.

Fax modems can also be used to send information from a computer to a distant fax machine. The information must be either an image or a text file that is stored in the computer. After appropriate software converts the file to a format compatible with fax machines, the distant fax machine is dialed and the file is transmitted. At the other end, the image of the page comes out of the receiving fax in the usual manner.

Combination fax modems cost only a little more than standard modems. They represent a good investment for people who do not already own a standard fax machine and who are likely to send only documents created on their computers. A fax modem cannot be used to send a copy of something already in print form, such as a birth certificate. There is simply no direct way to feed the piece of paper into the modem (unless you scan it in). Anything that is to be sent by a fax modem must first exist as a computer file.

Conclusion

This chapter examined a variety of technology applications that use data telecommunications techniques. The variety of applications for data telecommunications is almost unlimited. It is now possible to consult libraries around the world through Internet, bank on national holidays, and send a message to a traveling marketing representative, even if you do not have the faintest idea where that person is at the moment. With telecommunications, groups of people, separated by local, state, or even national boundaries, can work together to solve common problems.

Telecommunications Resources

America Online (Integrated services vendor), 8619 Westwood Center Drive, Vienna, VA 22182, 800-827-6364

CompuServe (Integrated services vendor), 5000 Arlington Center Boulevard, P.O. Box 20212, Columbus, OH 43220, 800-848-8199

Crosstalk (Communications software), Digital Communications Associates Inc., 1000 Alderman Drive, Alpharetta, GA 30202, 800-348-3221

Delphi (Integrated services vendor), 1030 Massachusetts Avenue, Cambridge, MA 02138, 800-695-4005

DIALOG (Database vendor), 3460 Hillview Avenue, Palo Alto, CA 94304, 800-334-2564

GEnie (Integrated services vendor), GE Information Services, P.O. Box 6403, Rockville, MD 20850, 301-340-4000

International Internet Association (Not-for-profit organization), 2020 Pennsylvania Avenue NW, Suite 852, Washington, DC 20006, 800-669-4780

MicroPhone Pro (Communications software), Software Ventures, Inc., 2907 Claremont Avenue, Berkeley, CA 94705, 510-644-3232

PCBoard (BBS software), Clark Development Co., Inc., P.O. Box 571365, Murray, UT 84157, 800-356-1686

Procomm Plus (Communications software), Datastorm Technologies, Inc., 3212 Lemone Industrial Boulevard, Columbia, MO 65201, 800-315-3282

Prodigy (Integrated services vendor), 445 Hamilton Avenue, White Plains, NY 10601, 800-776-3449

RBBS-PC (BBS software), Capital PC User Group Software Library, P.O. Box 1785, West Bethesda, MD 20827, 301-762-6775

Smartcom II (Communications software), Hayes Microcomputer Products, Inc., P.O. Box 105203, Atlanta, GA 30348, 404-441-1617

TBBS (BBS software), eSoft, Inc., 15200 East Girard Avenue, Aurora, CO 80014, 303-699-6565

White Knight (Communications software), FreeSoft Company, 105 McKinley Road, Beaver Falls, PA 15010, 412-846-2700

Word Perfect/Novell Application Group, 1555 North Technology Way, Orem, UT 84057, 800-321-4566

ZTerm (Communications software), Dave Alverson, 5635 Cross Creek Court, Mason, OH 45040

Recommended Reading

ATM networking: Increasing performance on the network. 1994. *Syllabus HEPC* 3(7): 12-14.

Beyda, W. J. 1989. *Basic data communications: A comprehensive overview*. Englewood Cliffs, NJ: Prentice-Hall.

Bowen, C., and D. Peyton. 1988. *The complete electronic bulletin board starter kit*. Des Plaines, IL: Bantam.

Buchanan, L. 1994. Connecting to the world: Getting your school on the Internet. *Multimedia Schools* 1(1): 14-20.

Bunch, R. M. 1993. Everything you always wanted to know about fiber optics but were afraid to ask. *Technos* 2(1): 13-15.

Campbell, G., and J. Heim. 1993. The best of online services [Guide to online services with related articles on online services, bulletin board systems, and Internet]. *PC World* (10) (October 11): 224.

Caputo, A. 1994. Seven secrets of searching: How and when to choose online. *Multimedia Schools* 1(1): 29-33.

Conhaim, W. W. 1991. Bulletin boards: A hidden resource for small business. *LINK-UP* 8(2): 16-17.

Derfler, F. J., Jr. 1992. Modem communication software: Too hard to use? *PC Magazine* 11(12).

Dutcher, W. 1993. How to retrofit a LAN to access the Internet. *PC Week* 10(45): 1.

Frisbie, A., J. Repman, and R. Price. 1991. Establishing an electronic bulletin board system. *Educational Technology* 31(4): 41-43.

Gonzalez, S. 1993. Using the Internet's resources. *Corporate Computing* 2(6) (June): 157.

Grosch, A. N. 1991. Bulletin board analysis: Select BBS software to fit your needs. *LINK-UP* 8(2): 14-15.

Hudspeth, D. 1990. The electronic bulletin board: Appropriate technology. *Educational Technology* 30(7): 40-43.

The Internet: Mining for information. 1993. *Higher Education Product Companion* 2(3): 32-34.

Jorgenson, T. 1990. The benefits of expensive timeshare systems with none of the expense! *Remark* 3: 7-10.

Lange, C. 1994. Privacy in the digital age. *NewMedia* 4(4): 65-68.

LaQuey, T. 1993. *Internet companion: A beginner's guide to global networking*. Reading, MA: Addison-Wesley.

Lawton, G. 1994. Education navigating superhighway potholes. *Communications Industries Report* 11(2): 1.

Lee, L. 1994. Internet expedition maps. *NewMedia* 4(4): 80-81.

Lewis, J. E. 1993. And they're off; the race to fiber optics. *Technos* 2(1): 8-12.

Magidson, S. 1993. On the quest for portable connectivity. *LAN Times* 10(5): 50.

Mostafa, J., T. Newell, and R. Trenthem. 1994. *The Easy Internet Handbook*. Castle Rock, CO: Hi Willow Research and Publishing.

Nimersheim, J. 1993. Extend control over your modem. *PC Computing* 6(5): 270-71.

Press, L. 1993. The Internet and interactive television. *Communications of the ACM* 36(12): 19-23.

Reinhardt, A. 1994. Building the data highway. *Byte* (March): 46-60.

Salemi, J. 1991. Tools for wide-area communications. *PC Magazine* 10(15): 231-300.

Skipton, C., et al. 1994. Internet expedition maps. *NewMedia* 4(4): 80-81.

Stump, L. 1993. Welcome to cyberspace. *EXE* 8(1): 65.

Telecommunications: The most complete guide ever. 1992. *Electronic Learning* 11(6): 18-29.

Tetzeli, R. 1994. Is going online worth the money? *Fortune* 129(12): 104-8.

Ubois, J. 1993. Where to look before you pick up the phone. *MacWEEK* 7(26): 42.

Vaughan-Nichols, S. J. 1993. The Internet connection: with a few tips, you can master the method of Internet madness. *Computer Shopper* 3(3): 724.

Wasson, G. 1993. The best connections. [Communications software]. *MacUser* 9(7): 218.

Worthington, S. L. S. 1994. Imaging on the Internet: Scientific/industrial resources. *Advanced Imaging* 9(2): 17-25.

7

Teleconferencing and Distance Education

An '80s Scenario

It was March, and Jim's mind was on San Diego. Next week he would be there with about 50 other executives from his company's branch offices around the country. He knew that he would have to sit through a number of boring training sessions, but he also knew that he would be able to sneak away for several mornings of golf. Jim was already planning his evenings based upon his prior experiences with the city's theme parks and restaurants.

The conference was scheduled at the premier hotel in the area, and Jim was surprised when he saw just how much his company was paying for his room. By the time the first-class air fare, conference fees, and a healthy per diem were factored in, Jim's company would be spending thousands of dollars for his week of training. He was a bit disappointed that the company refused to cover his green's fees or tourist attraction tickets this year, but he was told that times were tight, and the company had to save money wherever possible.

A '90s Scenario

The layoffs had been sweeping. When the merger took place, all branch offices had taken major hits, and Jim felt lucky to still have a job. Mid-level executives had been some of the major targets, and Jim had escaped only because his office was highly productive, but understaffed, before the cuts took place. While he had complained bitterly just months earlier that his office deserved at least three additional management positions, Jim now realized that the understaffing of his office had almost certainly saved his job. His future was still uncertain, though. Company goals for the next year required major increases in productivity. Jim's office was closer to those new goals than many of the others, but he knew the next wave of competition would be intense.

The new corporate headquarters considered training to be one of the most cost-effective methods of improving productivity, and they offered a variety of training sessions for all levels of employees. But there were no first-class tickets. In fact there were no airline tickets at all, and there were no week-long junkets. When employees went on golfing trips now, they were expected to use vacation days.

Instead, a small room in the office building had been remodeled into a self-contained teleconferencing training environment. A high technology two-way video delivery system capable of serving small groups had been installed. Microphones were carefully positioned to accommodate up to a dozen individuals. Computers, projection equipment, and electronic whiteboards were distributed throughout the room. The training sessions originated halfway across the country at the corporate headquarters, and employees from branches all across the nation participated.

This was indeed a new world for Jim. He quickly realized that the quality of the training was excellent, and he developed a management plan that provided incentives and rewards for all of his employees who participated in training components. At first, he found that his employees were apprehensive about the new training method, because they had never been involved in distance education. After they became familiar with the technique, Jim was pleased with their improving attitudes and the measurable productivity increases.

* * * *

Teleconferencing has been used for specialized purposes in business and industry for decades. When teleconferencing is mentioned, many people think of high-level, executive decision-making meetings. However, while teleconferencing is still used for this purpose, it has also spread to the mainstream of general training. Improvements in the technologies, a need to reduce overall costs, and observable increases in productivity have all lead to what is turning into a revolution in training. This chapter explores how teleconferencing techniques contribute to distance education with the following topics:

- An introduction to the three most common teleconferencing technologies
- Audio teleconferencing
- Audiographic teleconferencing
- Video teleconferencing
- Digital data lines

Introduction

While it is possible to deliver distance education by sending out work-books or videotapes, these approaches provide such limited opportunity for interaction that their effectiveness is often low. Teleconferencing provides the live, one-on-one, audiovisual communication that is so often necessary for effective training. Unfortunately, when compared with other training techniques, teleconferencing may seem complex, difficult to administer, and expensive. Recent advances in technology, though, are creating more practical teleconferencing options for lifelong learning applications. Three distinct categories of teleconferencing technologies are considered in this chapter.

Audio teleconferencing. This is the most mature of the techniques. Very little equipment is required, but as its name implies, it is limited to voice communications.

Audiographic teleconferencing. Computer and facsimile technologies are added to audio teleconferencing to allow figures, charts, and still pictures to be exchanged during the conference. The interactive exchange of images enhances the expression of ideas during the training process.

Video teleconferencing. This technology combines full-motion video with audio. It is useful for situations in which the use of motion enhances the course content. Most forms of video teleconferencing currently require careful cost justification in the training environment, but recent advances promise a variety of cost-effective applications in the near future.

Most forms of distance education use one or more of the three types of teleconferencing. Because of the significant difference in costs and perform-ance of these forms of teleconferencing, each deserves closer attention.

Audio Teleconferencing

Audio teleconferencing is noted for its simplicity, its adaptability, and its relatively low cost. Although some of the equipment, such as speaker-phones and directional microphones, has become more sophisticated over the years, the primary component of audio teleconferencing remains the inexpen-sive and common dial-up telephone line.

The only required additions to a standard conference room to use audio teleconferencing are a telephone line and a speakerphone. If the conference room is large, or if considerable interaction is expected, a system with an amplified speaker and multiple microphones may be useful. Sound-absorbing materials, such as an acoustic ceiling or draperies, greatly reduce the "talking in a barrel" distortion that often degrades a speakerphone conversation.

Audio teleconferencing can be quite simple, such as a conference-call on a telephone line, or it can be more complicated, such as an audio bridge that allows a dozen sales managers, each at separate locations, to hold a group meeting.

Speakerphones

The common speakerphone is a *simplex* message device. In other words, it does not allow simultaneous two-way conversations as does an ordinary telephone. People at both ends of the connection cannot transmit simultaneously. This process is similar to water flowing through a pipe. The water can go in either direction, but it can flow in only one direction at any time.

An ordinary telephone handset is a *duplex* message device. A standard handset is more like a water system with two pipes: one pipe for water going each direction. In a standard telephone handset, the earpiece and the microphone are sufficiently separated to prevent sounds coming through the earpiece from feeding back into the mouthpiece.

When a person's voice is coming through a speakerphone, however, the speakerphone must turn off its microphone. If it is not turned off, the incoming sound will be picked up by the microphone and almost instantly routed back to the person originating the message. At the least, this creates a strong echo of the speaker's voice. More likely, it will cause a feedback squeal similar to that generated when a microphone is too close to a loudspeaker in a public address system.

When the distant person pauses, or when someone at the receiving end talks loudly, the speakerphone switches off its speaker and activates its microphone. At this point, the voice of the distant person is cut off, and the flow reverses so that the distant person can hear what is being said in the classroom. Modern speakerphones are capable of making these simplex changes in direction so quickly that they are usually only a minor distraction. As people become familiar with the limitations of a speakerphone, they learn to establish a pattern of brief pauses during interactive discussions to prevent the loss of parts of the spoken message.

Full duplex audio teleconferencing speakerphone technologies are becoming more accessible. At present, though, such systems cost close to a thousand dollars because of the sophisticated electronic systems required to allow both microphone and speaker to remain active at all times. When a full duplex speakerphone is used in a classroom designed to minimize echoes, conversations can flow as easily as they can through regular telephone handsets.

Audio teleconferencing can be further complicated by long-distance telephone communications that are routed through satellites. When this happens, delays from a quarter second to a second may occur as the signals travel back and forth across these large distances. These delays, combined with simplex speakerphones, can cause awkward false starts in conversations. If satellite links are used in an audio teleconference, longer pauses must be built into the conversation.

Telephone Bridges

Many telephone lines have simple conference-calling features that make it easy to connect three locations. A person with a conference-calling telephone system simply dials the other two locations, and with the press of a button, all three are interconnected. If speakerphones are used at all three locations, the volumes may have to be adjusted so that they are evenly balanced. If either of the other people involved in the call also has conference-calling, then it is possible to tie in, or *daisychain*, additional locations. However, this process often results in audio levels too low for comfortable use.

When more than three locations must be connected in a teleconferencing process, the best solution is the use of a technology called a *telephone bridge*. The bridge is an electronic system that links multiple telephone lines and automatically balances the audio levels. The bridge can be rented from a telephone or long-distance company, or it can be owned and operated by the business itself. Unless a bridge is used several times a day, it is usually more economical to rent one.

A telephone bridge does not require any classroom equipment other than a standard telephone line. The actual bridge system is located at the telephone company, or in the case of a privately owned system, at the business switchboard. In any case, prior arrangements must be made to reserve the bridge for the time of the conference.

A bridge can be either *call-in* or *call-out*. With a call-in bridge, participants are given the bridge telephone number ahead of time, and they call the number at the beginning of the conference. The bridge system automatically connects the calls to the conference. A call-out bridge requires an operator to dial the telephone numbers of all the locations that will participate in the conference. As each number is reached, it becomes connected to the conference.

Each of these techniques has strengths and weaknesses. The call-in technique allows individuals to call from any location, and a participant can enter the conference late or reenter the conference if accidentally disconnected. The bridge telephone number can be set to remain open during the entire meeting. On the other hand, the conference must be planned far enough in advance to distribute the telephone number for the bridge, and the individual participants will be charged for any long-distance fees that might apply.

The call-out process does not require advance distribution of a telephone number for the bridge. In fact, most telephone companies and long-distance services offer on-demand call-out bridge systems that can be operated with a touch-tone telephone. In these systems, the conference leader calls the bridge management system and then uses an automated process to enter the telephone numbers to be connected for the conference. With a call-out system, all charges for the conference, including long-distance fees, are billed to the conference leader's telephone number. One major disadvantage of a call-out system is that it is difficult for a participant to enter the conference late or to be reconnected if accidentally disconnected during the conference.

Words of Advice

Audio teleconferencing is the most economical method available for interactive distance education. The strength of the technology is attributed to the extensive telephone network in the United States and many other countries. The greatest weakness of the method is the inability to include visual information. Practical experience has also shown that audio-only communication is stressful for many learners. An audio teleconference lesson should contain short (not more than 15 minutes) segments of audio interaction intermixed with other activities. Finally, prepare any handouts or other visual materials that might be of value during the presentation in advance. Distribute these materials ahead of time so they will be ready for the group.

Audiographic Teleconferencing

Audiographic teleconferencing adds two-way image transmission to audio teleconferencing. Modern equipment allows non-motion color images to be sent from one location to another in seconds. A variety of equipment choices are available to create or capture the image at the site where it originates and to display the image at the distant location.

The addition of graphics to an audio conference allows the exchange of spontaneously drawn sketches or illustrations. It is much easier to show an image of a complex formula than it is to describe it. Similarly, it is easier to discuss an organizational chart when everyone in the conversation can see it. The graphics devices can also eliminate the need to distribute overhead projection images or slides before the teleconference. Instead, each graphic is transmitted to the remote sites while it is displayed by the conference leader.

Facsimile Machines

The most basic equipment needed for an audiographic teleconference is a pair of facsimile machines plus the speakerphones used in a standard audio teleconference. (See chapter 6 for more information about facsimile machines.) The fax machines allow paper sketches to be sent back and forth during the conference. To avoid interruptions in the audio, the fax machines should be assigned dedicated telephone lines.

Fax machines, like many other audiographic devices, are designed to work in pairs, so the fax machine at the originating site must send the image to each of the other sites involved in the teleconference one at a time. Newer fax machines allow the creation of mailing lists, so all of the teleconference sites can be sent the same image in quick succession. The use of faxes at multiple sites mandates that each site have one line for the telephone and a separate line for the fax; otherwise, the interruptions in the conversation as images are sent to and from the multiple locations would become too distracting.

Microcomputers

Audiographic teleconferencing is one of the most rapidly evolving fields of distance education. Although fax machines can be used to supply basic graphic capabilities, microcomputers and related peripherals have become the primary vehicles of audiographic teleconferencing.

A microcomputer used for audiographic teleconferencing uses a color display system connected to a large classroom monitor or a projection system. The computer also contains a video capture card connected to one or more external video cameras (See chapter 3 for more information about video capture cards). One of these cameras, mounted on a copy stand, could provide controls for zooming in and out or focusing on the documents placed on the stand. A mouse or graphics tablet allows the creation of freehand drawings and positions a pointer on a captured video image. Finally, the computer must contain a high-speed modem, fax-modem, or digital link that connects the system to the telephone line. The images used during the teleconference are sent or received through the modem (See chapter 6 for more information on modems).

Although these hardware components have been available for several years, convenient software that integrates the hardware into a complete audiographic system is only now becoming available. Many computer-based audiographic systems use custom-developed software or collections of commercial programs that are still not fully integrated. As software improves, it will be much easier for teleconference participants to select or prepare appropriate illustrations as an audiographic conference is taking place. At present, participants must be well trained in the use of the systems and must prepare most materials before the conference.

Words of Advice

Audiographic teleconferencing is a compromise between inexpensive, but visually limited, audio-only teleconferencing techniques and the more costly and complex motion video techniques. If the intended lessons can benefit from the interactive use of still visuals, and only two sites are involved, then audiographic techniques are the best choice. Because this technology is currently going through such dynamic development, it is impossible to recommend specific hardware and software; however, common sense should be used when trying to match systems to applications. Some of the following factors should be considered.

Number of simultaneous sites. Most audiographic systems connect only two sites. If equipment is advertised as being able to connect more than two sites, ask for demonstrations to see how easy it is to exchange images among the sites.

Speed of image transmission. It usually takes from 15 seconds to a minute to send a copy of a screen or page through a standard modem or fax machine.

Resolution of images. The greater the detail or resolution of the transmitted image, the longer it takes to transmit it via a computer or modem. It gains nothing to send images in greater detail than can be displayed at the other end. If a projection system can display only 16-color images, there is no point in sending pictures with 256 colors. The pictures with more colors will take longer to send but will not look any better on the limited projection system.

Type of telephone line(s) required. Nearly all audiographic systems require one or two standard dial-up telephone lines. A few systems require special direct dial or leased telephone lines. Because of the differences in cost, ensure that any additional benefits offered by leased line systems are essential before committing to the expense.

Video Teleconferencing

Full motion video teleconferencing is the closest option to actually having a group in one location. A common form of video teleconferencing is one-way video with two-way audio. The video image is distributed from the teleconference leader's site through cable, microwave, or satellite technology to the distant sites, while the two-way audio is managed with a standard telephone bridge.

This is the method of choice for many business, military, and industrial training programs. While it is expensive, it is far less so than transporting people from all over the country to one location for training. New technologies such as desktop video teleconferencing are reducing the costs of video teleconferencing to the point where even small companies are able to use it.

Analog Video Transmission

Analog television delivery is one of the oldest, most widely available techniques for video teleconferencing. Analog video technology has been in use for decades, and is the standard form of video transmission, so all televisions are designed to receive analog signals. The television programs that come from broadcast towers, standard cable systems, educational microwave systems, and satellite dishes are all analog signals, although their individual characteristics may vary. While broadcast television may have little to offer to the company interested in the use of video teleconferencing for training, the other analog technologies do provide several options.

Cable Television

Most cable television systems allow educational institutions to transmit television courses over their networks. In some areas, universities use this technique to offer informal or formal education courses to the community at large. This is most effective in areas where a high percentage of the community subscribes to the cable television system.

Course distribution through cable television is a cost-effective means of training. In most cases, the only cost to a company is the tuition required for employees to receive formal credit. In the case of informal education courses, there may be no costs at all. A few cable companies are also exploring true interactive teleconferencing by using telephone bridges to establish two way audio communications with live instructors. These courses are normally offered through a local community college or university.

Cable Television Advances

Cable television companies are currently engaged in a heated battle with telephone companies to provide digital data to customers. Telephone companies seek to provide video services traditionally offered by cable companies, and cable companies seek to provide communications services formerly provided by telephone companies. If communications systems are deregulated, the distinctions between cable TV and telephone systems will blur. Much of this battle has been brought about by the new technologies for digitizing voice and video into data, as will be discussed later in this chapter.

Cable companies will soon be able to use the technology of digital data to offer hundreds of channels to each home and office. While many of these channels will be devoted to commercial entertainment purposes, a larger number of channels will be available for interactive training. If cable and telephone companies become less regulated, then it is possible that interactive training classes with two-way video and two-way audio can be delivered through a single provider.

Microwave Television Conferencing

Microwave transmissions provide a cost-effective method for educational applications of video teleconferencing over more localized areas. Most microwave systems are designed to transmit video signals to areas less than 20 miles apart. The most popular systems use microwave frequencies designated by the Federal Communications Commission (FCC) as Instructional Television Fixed Service (ITFS) stations. ITFS stations operate at a lower power than satellite or commercial broadcast television, making the transmission equipment relatively inexpensive. Reception equipment is also relatively inexpensive as long as the receiving sites are located within 20 miles of the transmitter and there are no hills or tall buildings to block the signal.

ITFS is popular with community colleges and universities as a method of distributing courses throughout communities. By using pairs of ITFS channels, two-way video teleconferencing can be set up between a main campus classroom and a branch campus classroom. One drawback of microwave ITFS communication, however, is the limited number of channels available in any one area. Many metropolitan areas already have all available channels in use, so no further expansion of ITFS teleconferencing is possible.

Analog Satellite Transmissions

Satellites enhance the use of analog video for teleconferencing by transmitting the signal over much greater distances than is possible using broadcast towers or independent cable systems. Two distinct sets of equipment are needed for satellite systems. The *uplink* is the set of equipment needed to create and transmit the signal to the satellite. The *downlink* is the equipment needed to receive and display the signal.

A studio conference room is needed at the origination site. This room must be properly wired for the lighting, microphones, and cameras necessary to produce the training program. The studio is connected to a control room where one or more technicians control the television cameras and microphones. The resulting video signal is connected to an uplink transmitter and a large satellite dish beams the signal up to the satellite. Uplink transmitters and dishes are very expensive and are often leased.

Video satellites can handle many channels, called transponders, at one time. However, each conference must be assigned a specific satellite and transponder for the time slot that the conference will cover. The owners of the satellites coordinate the reservations and collect the usage fees.

The most critical part of a downlink is the receiving dish antenna. These dishes, common in backyards, select and amplify the desired satellite signals. Each distant site must have a satellite receiving dish with the appropriate electronics to select and amplify the television signal. The signal is fed into the conference rooms, where it is displayed on standard television monitors or projection systems. In regular satellite transmissions, the outgoing audio is combined with the picture much as it is in commercial broadcasts. The distant conference rooms have an audio teleconferencing system to allow participants at each distant site to have audio interaction with the instructor or other participants.

Satellite video conferencing is expensive, and it is not cost-effective for most businesses to purchase uplinks to originate conferences. Instead, many companies set up microwave or cable connections to a local site where they can lease time on an uplink as needed. Downlinks, on the other hand, have become inexpensive and common. Many companies purchase downlinks and use them on a regular basis to receive video conferences from headquarters and university courses for their employees.

Digital Video Teleconferencing

Although satellite is the most common method for long-distance distribution of video teleconferencing, alternate techniques have been developed in an effort to reduce the cost of video teleconferencing. Almost all of the newer techniques convert the video images into digital signals. Computers or proprietary hardware process and compress the pictures so that they can be transmitted by more cost-effective methods, such as telephone digital data lines. Digital data lines will be covered in detail later in the chapter.

Many digital systems are packaged into proprietary portable carts. These carts often contain monitors, cameras, and microphones so they can transmit and receive digitized video. Such systems can be used to create two-way video and audio teleconferences. If more than two sites are involved, however, these systems can become very complicated. Standards are slowly evolving for high-quality, digitized video, but at the present many systems are incompatible with each other.

Digital Telecommunications Equipment

The equipment used for digital teleconferencing is similar to that used in analog teleconferencing. The cameras, monitors, and audio equipment are the same as in regular analog studios. However, all digital video teleconferencing systems use a device called a video *codec* to interconnect the data line and the video equipment. A codec digitizes and compresses a video signal prior to sending it through a data line. All sites connected to the line need a compatible codec to decompress the signal and turn it back into a standard analog video signal for television monitors and projection systems. (See chapter 3 for more information on codecs.)

Desktop Video Teleconferencing on Computer Networks

A few years ago, only proprietary systems costing hundreds of thousands of dollars could provide digitized video teleconferencing. Now powerful microcomputers are capable of controlling inexpensive video teleconferencing codec boards, and the age of desktop video teleconferencing has arrived. This technology is still in its infancy, but it will almost certainly become a major force in business and training applications. Several companies, using both MS-DOS and Macintosh computers, have demonstrated systems that are able to capture and transmit a small, live image to a computer screen at another location. A typical configuration for desktop video includes a video digitizing board, communications board, a small video camera, a microphone, and a speaker (See fig. 7.1). The rapidly dropping costs of this technology will make it an appealing alternative to full-scale video teleconferencing.

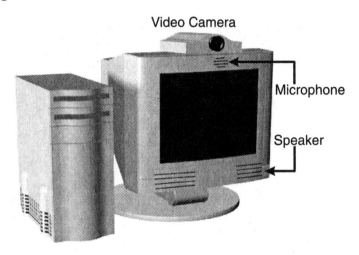

Video Camera

Microphone

Speaker

Fig. 7.1. Desktop video teleconferencing system.

At present, there are some limitations to desktop video systems. First, most systems transmit the images at 15 frames per second, half the normal video speed. This may cause the motion to appear jerky. For many video conferencing applications, this is not a major limitation.

A second restriction concerns the method of connecting the computers. A high speed LAN can be used within a building, but telephone lines are used for longer distances. Most inexpensive systems have been demonstrated using Integrated Services Digital Network (ISDN) lines. Because most telephone companies are only now beginning to upgrade to ISDN lines, desktop video systems might be limited to localized applications for several years.

Desktop video teleconferencing is now being used within companies where a large number of people are connected to a high speed LAN or WAN. Most desktop video equipment and software manufacturers recommend that the network deliver at least 10 to 16 megabits per second (Mbps) to each video-capable workstation and that all trunk lines that interconnect buildings or file servers operate at a minimum of 100 Mbps. Many older LANs can not operate at these speeds, so converting to desktop teleconferencing might carry with it significant system modernization costs.

Words of Advice

Video teleconferencing offers the highest level of information exchange of the three forms of teleconferencing. Audio, color, and motion images can be exchanged. However, some forms of video teleconferencing are still very expensive and impractical for small businesses. The most affordable and accessible video techniques include the use of ISDN lines for partial motion; commercial satellite courses to provide training that is unavailable at the job site; and standard satellite (one way video, two way audio) teleconferencing. Each of these applications requires careful planning. In particular, the following details should be considered.

Justification. Video teleconferencing involves significant financial and personnel resources. Prior to finalizing these commitments, careful evaluations should be conducted to ensure that employee productivity or moral will benefit from the changes.

Physical Facilities. Regular conference rooms can be adapted to receive video teleconferencing, but a special facility for originating video conferences will probably have to be constructed. The special requirements for the cameras, lighting, and sound systems often exceed what can be accomplished through minor renovations of traditional conference rooms. An expert should be consulted prior to developing a studio room.

Training the trainers. Most trainers need to be taught how to teach in front of cameras. It takes training and practice to know which camera is active, how much to gesture, and how to prepare visual materials. If trainers are expected to teach video classes, they should be reinforced with the proper training.

Alternate Planning. No matter how carefully the video teleconference is planned, things can go wrong. A cable might be accidentally cut at a construction site, or a sudden storm might twist your satellite dish out of position. These possibilities emphasize the importance of having an alternate plan to cover the situation. In most cases, a standard telephone bridge is sufficient to provide a two-way audio backup.

Digital Data Lines

Telephone data lines are designed to transmit digitized information more efficiently than standard audio telephone lines. Digital data lines are important for interconnecting LANs into wide area networks and for videographic and video teleconferencing.

The standard telephone line transmits a continuous range of audio frequencies and volumes that are optimized for the reproduction of human voices. Because continuous ranges of frequencies are involved, these telephone lines are called dial-up analog lines. As covered in chapter 6, modems translate computer data into audio tones that can be transmitted through standard analog telephone lines. However, modems reach their limits at around 20 to 30 kilobits per second (Kbps)—too slow to transmit motion video.

Telephone companies and other vendors provide a variety of communication services beyond the basic dial-up voice lines. Many of these services are digital rather than analog and allow data to be transmitted a higher speeds than the analog lines. In general, these services fall into three categories: circuit switched, leased line, and packet switched. These communication lines can transmit data at rates from 20 Kbps to 45 Mbps. The higher transmission rates are important because they allow digitized video and audio to be transmitted from place to place in direct competition with satellite video transmission.

Circuit Switched Systems

Circuit switched digital systems are the most like standard telephone lines. A set monthly fee provides access to the system and additional fees accumulate as the system is used. In most cases, a dial-up process connects the sites. There are two common digital circuit switched systems. The oldest is the 56 Kbps line used exclusively for computer data transfer. These systems cost about $50 a month plus $.08 to $.30 per minute for use. Switched 56 lines are used mainly by businesses to interconnect small LANs into a WAN.

The second type of circuit switched system is an evolving standard called Integrated Services Digital Network (ISDN). These digital systems are designed to handle both voice and data in a variety of combinations. ISDN requires system-wide upgrades to a telephone network, but it has the potential of bringing true digital transmission to every home and business in the nation. The standard ISDN telephone line has two 64 Kbps channels and one 16 Kbps channel. The 16 Kbps channel is used by the system to control the other two channels, so it is not available for sending or receiving information. The 64 Kbps channels, on the other hand, can be combined into one 128 Kbps channel for computer data, or they can be kept separate so that one channel can transmit digitized voice while the other transmits data.

ISDN has great potential in that it can use the copper telephone wire system currently in place. But to implement ISDN on a large scale, telephone companies will need to upgrade switching equipment, and homes and businesses will need to upgrade their telephones and computer interfaces. This transition will occur gradually as older equipment reaches the end of its useful life.

Currently, ISDN availability and costs vary dramatically. In some areas, ISDN lines are available for nearly the same cost as standard voice lines, but in other areas they are not yet available, or they might add $40 to $50 to the monthly telephone bill. Costs and availability are expected to stabilize over the next several years.

Leased Lines

If a company requires 24-hour-a-day access to computers or videoconferencing in branch offices, leased data lines might be the most sensible route. A leased data line is a constant, private connection between two points. There is no need to dial a number to connect to the distant point because the line continuously links the two points together.

While it is possible to lease common voice lines, there is no technical and little economic advantage to doing this. Instead, much higher performance digital data lines are usually leased. The two most common types of leased lines are T1 and T3, and the capabilities of these lines are incredible.

T1 leased digital lines. A standard T1 line allows digital information to be transmitted at 1.544 Mega (million) bits per second (Mbps). This is a transmission speed 160 times faster than a 9,600 bps modem! The standard T1 line can transmit digitized video conferences, although video compression techniques are still needed. T1 lines are also commonly used to link large local LANs into a powerful WAN. Large amounts of data can flow through such a linkage, so the entire system can appear to function very smoothly.

Performance has its price, however. Distance is a primary factor in the cost of a leased T1 line, and a transcontinental T1 line can easily cost $20,000 per month. This might seem astounding to the average business person, but consider the cost of keeping 160 long distance lines open for 24 hours a day for one month! That cost could exceed one million dollars per month!

T3 leased digital lines. If T1 lines do not provide enough data power, there is an even faster alternative—the T3 line. This leased line can transmit data at 44.736 Mbps. This is roughly equivalent to 29 simultaneous T1 lines!

The price of T3 lines can easily exceed $100,000 per month, so there are not very many of them in use. Probably the primary user of T3 lines is the government, which uses T3 interconnections for the super computers that make up our defense and research backbones.

Circuit switched leased digital lines. Few companies can afford or justify 100 percent use of T1 or T3 lines; however, many companies have times when they could make a short-term use of one of these lines for a teleconference or a large data transfer. Vendors have quickly caught on to the transient data needs of businesses and have started renting out their leased T1 and T3 lines. The vendors also rent the equipment needed to make the necessary connections, and they supply technical support during the time the line is in use. After a business signs a contract with one of the vendors, access to the T1 or T3 line is controlled by a circuit switched process, much like an ISDN line.

While the vendor adds enough to the basic cost of the line to make a profit, it is still reasonable for a company to use a leased line vendor if such a line is needed only an hour or two each week. For example, a teleconference can be much less expensive (and more secure) when transmitted over a leased digital line than when sent up to a satellite.

Packet Switched Lines

Circuit switched and leased lines are most useful when two locations must be interconnected. If more than two locations must share information, the third alternative, a packet switched line, is sometimes more effective. As the name implies, data are broken into packets; each packet contains specific information regarding its origination site, destination site, and age.

A packet switched line might be shared by several businesses at once, but the imbedded information in each packet insures that it arrives at the correct location. As the packets arrive, they are reassembled into their original form.

During periods of light usage, packet switched lines can transfer data to and from multiple locations at speeds comparable to those of circuit switched and leased lines. Costs range from $500 to $2,000 a month, depending on the distances, number of sites, and amount of usage.

Because of the flexible nature of packet switching, variations can occur in transmission speeds during busy times of the day. For this reason, this technology might not work effectively for digital video teleconferencing. There could be times when gaps occur in the motion video and sound when packets are delayed briefly due to heavy line usage. See figure 7.2 for a comparison of telephone data lines.

	Speed	Cost per month	Primary Use	Access
56 Kbps Line	56 Kbps	$50-$100	Data	Dial-up
ISDN	128 Kbps	$35 - $100	Voice/Data	Dial-up
T1	1.544 Mbps	$20,000	Data/Video	Point to Point
T3	44.736 Mbps	$100,000	Data/Video	Point to Point
Packet Switched	Varies	$500 - $2000	Data	Multi-Point

Fig. 7.2. Comparison of telephone data lines with approximate costs.

Although there can be significant variations in the results, all forms of digital data lines can be used to send a video teleconference from one location to another. In general, the slower lines, such as ISDN, will be able to provide audio with a small, step-motion image. The fastest lines, such as a T3 line, will provide a video teleconference of a quality equal to that of a satellite transmission.

Conclusion

Audio, audiographic, and video teleconferencing have developed to the point where a number of techniques are now practical for businesses and universities. When properly integrated into an overall training program, these techniques can provide enhanced learning experiences to many employees. Figure 7.3 provides a summary of the characteristics of the teleconferencing techniques discussed in this chapter.

	Audio	Audiographic	Video Satellite	Video Desktop
Features	2-way audio	2-way audio 2-way images	2-way audio 1-way video	2-way audio 2-way video
Course Content	Highly Verbal	Verbal / Visual	Verbal / Visual	Verbal / Visual
Advance Planning	5 Days	1 month	3 months	None
Location	2 or more sites	2 sites	2 or more sites	2 or more sites
% of Total Class	10 - 15	30 - 60	75 - 100	N / A
Relative Costs	Low	Moderate	High	Moderate

Fig. 7.3. Characteristics of teleconferencing techniques.

Teleconferencing Resources

AT&T Global Business Video Services (AT&T Telemedia Personal Video System), Video Technical Service, 8100 E. Maplewood, Englewood, CO 80111, 800-VIDEO-GO

Compression Labs Inc. (Cameo Personal Video System), 2860 Junction Avenue, San Jose, CA 95134, 408-435-3000

EyeTel Communications (Communicator III), 267 W. Esplanade, North Vancouver, British Columbia, Canada V7M1A5, 800-736-3236

GPT Video Systems, Inc., 478 Wheelers Farms Road, Milford, CT 06460, 800-442-4788

Hitachi America Ltd. (Telecommunications Division), 3617 Parkway Lane, Norcross, GA 30092, 404-446-8820

IBM (Person to Person with Action Media II), 1133 Westchester Avenue, White Plains, NY 10604, 512-823-3258

InSoft (InSoft Communique!), InSoft Conference Kit, Executive Park West I, Suite 307, 4718 Old Gettysburg Road, Mechanicsburg, PA 17055, 717-730-9501

Instructional Television Consortium (ITC Catalog of Mass Media College Courses), American Association of Community and Junior Colleges, One Dupont Circle NW, Suite 410, Washington, DC 20036

Intel Corp. (Intel Proshare Personal Conferencing Video System), 2200 Mission College Boulevard, P.O. Box 58119, Santa Clara, CA 95052, 800-538-3373

InVision Systems Corp. (Desktop Videoconferencing), 8500 Leesburg Pike #300, Vienna, VA 22182, 703-506-0094

MRA Associates (VIDCall Personal Communication), 2102B Gallows Road, Vienna, VA 22182, 703-448-5373

Northern Telecom, Inc. (VISIT Video), Northern Telecom Plaza, 200 Athens Way, Nashville, TN 37228, 800-667-8437

Panasonic Communications & Systems Company, Two Panasonic Way, Secaucus, NJ 07094, 201-348-7000

PBS Adult Learning Service (The Guide), 1320 Braddock Place, Alexandria, VA 22314, 800-257-2578

PictureTel Corporation, The Tower at Northwoods, 222 Rosewood Drive, Danvers, MA 01923, 800-716-6000

ShareVision Technology Inc., 2951 Zanker Road, San Jose, CA 95134, 408-428-0330

Silicon Graphics, Inc. (Indigo Indy), 2011 N. Shoreline Boulevard, Mountain View, CA 94043, 800-800-7441

Sony Corporation of America (Conference & Satellite Systems), Business and Professional Group, 3 Paragon Drive, Montvale, NJ 07645, 201-930-7194

Specom Technologies, Corp. (Picfon System), 2322 Walsh Avenue, Santa Clara, CA 95051, 408-982-1880

Videoconferencing Systems Inc., 5801 Goshen Springs Road, Norcross, GA 30071, 404-242-7566

Viewpoint Systems (Personal Viewpoint), 2247 Wisconsin Street, Suite 110, Dallas, TX 75229, 214-243-0634

V-Tel Corporation, 108 Wild Basin Road, Austin, TX 78746, 512-314-2700

Recommended Reading

Arnold, K. 1993. A buyer's guide to desktop videoconferencing. *NewMedia* 3(11): 66-71.

Brown, E. 1994. Intel jumps into videoconferencing. *NewMedia* 4(4): 29.

Burruss, B. G. 1990. Resources for telecourses: A reference list. (ERIC Document Reproduction Service No. ED325103).

Carroll, J. R., and D. M. Robertson. 1993. Corporate training via videoconferencing; case studies and usage reports. *Teleconference* 12(2): 26-35.

Hargadon, T. 1992. Networked media sends a message. *NewMedia* 2(11): 26-29.

Herman, B. 1993. Welcome to the jungle. *Teleconnect* 11(2): 64(7).

Kuehn, T. 1989. Fax fever. *AV Communications* 23(5): 29-30.

Lambriola, D. 1994. Remote possibilities [Reviews of whiteboard software]. *PC Magazine* 13(11): 223(6).

Lauriston, R. 1993. Serving up video. *NewMedia* 3(11): 52-57.

Lindstrom, R. 1992. Shrinking the globe with videoconferencing. *Presentation Products Magazine* 6(6): 22-28.

Machrone, B. 1994. Seeing is almost believing [Reviews of desktop video teleconferencing software]. *PC Magazine* 13(11): 233(8).

Merwin, A. 1993. Videoconferencing goes to work. *NewMedia* 3(11): 60-64.

———. 1994. I see what you mean. *NewMedia* 20(4): 38-42.

Mirho, C. 1993. Reach out and touch someone's PC: The Windows Telephony API. *Microsoft Systems Journal* 8(12): 15(24).

Moeller, M. 1994. LANs and WANs: Collaborating to make better presentations. *Presentations* 8(4): 18-22.

———. 1994. Videoconferencing hits the desktop. *Presentations* 8(5): 16-20.

Nelson, L. J. 1994. The latest in compression hardware & software. *Advanced Imaging* 9(1): 56-60.

Ostendorf, V. A. 1990. Shopping for a satellite curriculum. *Media and Methods* 27(2): 10, 38-39.

Pohrte, T. W. 1990. Telecourses: Instructional design for nontraditional students. *New Directions for Community Colleges* 18(3): 55-61.

Press, L. 1993. The Internet and interactive television. *Communications of the ACM* 36(12): 19-24.

Price, M. A. 1991. Designing video classrooms. *Adult Learning* 2(4): 15-19.

Reveaux, T. 1992. Videoconferencing moves to the desktop. *NewMedia* 2(11): 33-35.

———. 1993. Learning goes the distance. *NewMedia* 3(7): 42-43.

Rhode, D. 1994. Time may be right for ISDN. *Network World* 11(14): 1(2).

Salemi, J. 1994. Let's Interface [Reviews of group conferencing software]. *PC Magazine* 13(11): 191(9).

Schnaidt, P. 1993. An ISDN issue. *LAN Magazine* 8(3): 21(2).

———. 1993. Dial-up internetworking. *LAN Magazine* 8(1): 21(2).

Schell, M. 1994. Image conferencing on the factory floor; now. *Advanced Imaging* 9(5): 42-46.

Shaeffer, J. M. 1990. Preparing faculty and designing courses for delivery via audio teleconferencing. *Journal of Adult Education* 18(2): 11-18.

Skipton, C. 1993. Low-cost videoconferencing systems arrive. *NewMedia* 3(7): 82.

Stump, L. 1993. Welcome to cyberspace. *EXE* 8(1): 65(4).

Verduin, J. R. 1991. *Distance education: The foundations of effective practice*. San Francisco: Jossey-Bass.

Development Software for Training Applications

A Scenario

The activities of the last half-hour appeared to have been an almost spontaneous interaction of people and technology. In brief, the executive board had met, considered and discussed a proposal, and approved it with minor variations. The approval process that normally took several months was completed within one scheduled meeting. Every executive at the meeting felt good about the decision to develop and implement the new electronic performance support system (PSS) for their electric power utility.

In reality, many hours of careful preparation led up to the successful meeting. The training and computing people met a number of times to evaluate new technologies that might improve the productivity of company employees. Once they made the decision to recommend a PSS, preparations began for the meeting to present the idea to the executive board.

It was decided that the first part of the presentation would be a linear briefing on current performance problems and the projected financial savings if those problems could be resolved. Because this was to be the opening presentation of the meeting, it had to be smooth and attention-getting. The board room had recently been renovated to accommodate electronic presentations, so a popular presentation software package was selected to deliver an electronic version of a multimedia slide show. Pictures were incorporated to illustrate some of the specific problem areas, and digital recordings of employee comments were used to emphasize some of the major issues.

The second part of the session included a simulation of a PSS. Because the PSS did not yet exist, a hypermedia program was used to create the simulation. With relatively little programming, it was possible to create a clear picture of how such a system would deliver computer-based instruction on an "as needed" basis. A variety of multimedia examples were also incorporated into the demonstration.

139

The final part of the meeting required reaching a consensus for the final structure and timetable of the proposed project. The team decided to use a decision support system to guide the executives through the process of reaching their final decisions. Outlines of the project were entered ahead of time and anticipated options were included. The board members had already used this system several times during brainstorming sessions, and they were familiar with the keyboards and monitors available to them.

The meeting was indeed a success. The initial presentation captured the interest of the executive board members and quickly apprised them of productivity problems. The simulation provided a clear understanding of the proposed solution to the problems, and the decision support software allowed the members to suggest changes that might enhance the system. After the meeting, several of the board members mentioned how pleased they were to see their ideas quickly blend into the overall plan.

* * * *

Presentation software, hypermedia development tools, authoring systems, decision support systems, expert systems, intelligent tutoring systems, and electronic performance support systems are rapidly evolving tools that have an impact on the design and delivery of instruction. This chapter provides an overview of the following topics:

- Presentation software

- Hypermedia development tools

- Authoring systems

- Expert systems

- Intelligent tutoring systems

- Electronic performance support systems

Introduction

A few years ago, it was easy for a computer programmer to impress an instructional design team. All that was needed was to use a few external calls in a program to animate the dials of a control panel or to create simple sounds from the computer's internal speaker. Soon, external control of commercial quality videotape and videodisc players became possible. Programmers and computer science engineers rallied to the cause, creating external interfaces and software routines to allow computers to control these devices.

The dam had broken. Following close behind simple interactive video was a flood of multimedia techniques and devices. New hardware made it possible to overlay video and computer information on the same screen. Video digitizers made it possible to capture an image and interweave it into a presentation. A variety of audio capture and playback alternatives became available. It soon became apparent that computer-based training was entering a new age. It was no longer possible to deal with all of the multimedia alternatives by simply adding external patches to traditional programming languages; whole new software development approaches were needed.

Presentation Software

Presentation software is designed for creating, developing, and delivering electronic versions of slide shows. The presentations are linear in format, and the computer is used to advance or back up through the slides during a presentation. Briefings, class lectures, and speeches often incorporate strategies appropriate to presentation software.

Presentation software became popular in business settings once computer technology was available in meeting rooms. Trainers quickly adopted this tool because they found that lecture notes and overhead transparencies were much easier to manage, revise, and deliver in electronic form.

There are many popular presentation software programs, including PowerPoint by Microsoft Corporation, Action by Macromedia, and Harvard Graphics by Software Publishing Corp. While commercial programs do not all have the same features, a typical development session might proceed as follows:

1. Decide on the look of the presentation.

    Most presentation programs have a number of pre-defined templates that can be applied. The templates determine the text fonts and sizes, background colors and patterns, and arrangement of information on the screen. The amount of information that can be placed on each slide varies according to the template, so it is a good idea to decide on the template before you start to prepare materials.

2. Collect text and images for the presentation.

    Either the presentation software or a standard word processing program can be used to organize the text that will accompany the slides. Simple images for the slides can be created within most commercial presentation products, but pictures or complex illustrations are best imported from external programs. Most programs include large libraries of clip art to enhance the slides.

3. Sequence the presentation.

Often slides are not created in the order in which they are to be shown because it saves time to create similar slides together. For example, all text slides might be created first, followed by the charts and graphs slides. After the slides are created, their order can be adjusted as needed by using an electronic slide table, a feature that allows a group of slides to be viewed in miniature. A mouse can be used to click and drag and drop slides into their new presentation order.

4. Add special effects.

One of the strengths of presentation software is the ability to create dynamic transitions between slides. Rather than one image simply replacing another, the new image can "push" the old one off the screen, "wipe" onto the screen, or evolve out of some geometric pattern. Transition effects have become common in commercial television, and conservative use adds a level of professionalism to presentations.

If a multimedia computer is used to create a presentation, sound and digitized motion images can often be added. There are wide variations in the amount of control provided by presentation software over these features. If multimedia effects are to be an integral part of presentations, the presentation software must be chosen very carefully. For example, some presentation packages allow a sound effect to begin only when the slide first appears. With this type of software, there is no way to delay a sound effect for a specified amount of time after the slide appears, making it difficult to combine animation and sound sequences.

5. Prepare for delivery.

Presentation software often provides a separate runtime program or viewer for the delivery of the show. The viewer is designed to provide a smooth delivery of the presentation, but it does not allow for changes in the presentation. In most cases, the software license allows the viewer and the presentation to be copied and distributed throughout the company. Licenses vary regarding commercial distribution, however. If you are planning to develop a commercial presentation for sale, you must clarify your distribution rights with the publisher of the presentation software.

Hypermedia Software

Presentation software is designed to produce linear presentations, but it is limited in its ability to create interactive courseware. For example, many presentation software packages do not provide a way to produce menu screens. As a result, open-ended "Choose what you would like to do. . ." presentations are not possible with most presentation software.

A second group of software products has evolved to fill the market for open-ended presentations. Commonly called *hypermedia* products, they provide multiple connected pathways through a body of information. Hypermedia allows a user to select *buttons* (active areas on the screen) that jump from one topic to related or supplementary material found in various forms, such as text, graphics, audio, or video. While running a program, an individual selects a button by mouse or by touch screen. The program instructions embedded in the button determine what happens next.

When compared with presentation software, hypermedia products such as ToolBook by Asymetrix, LinkWay by IBM, and HyperCard by Apple greatly expand the types of programs that can be created and delivered. Because these programs can branch, incorporate multimedia, and perform specialized tasks, a clearly defined design phase is an essential component of the development process. The following steps might be followed to create a hypermedia program.

1. Design the program.

   Hypermedia presentations are designed to allow individuals to choose alternative paths. Because one level of choices often leads to additional levels, careful planning is required in order to prevent time-consuming developmental mistakes. Flow charts and storyboards are generally used to define a program before actual development begins.

2. Create the base page.

   The screen background or "base page" is usually created first. This is similar to the template in presentation software in that it establishes the basic look of all other screens. Any buttons, such as "help" or "exit" that are added to the base automatically appear on all other screens.

3. Create screens and buttons in draft form.

   Next, create rough drafts of all screens and buttons. To save time, instead of typing all of the text on the screens, enter only critical information. If completed pictures are not yet available, use outlines or sketches. The intent is to get the program operational as quickly as possible so that the logic or flow can be tested.

   If the performance is to be delivered on a different computer than the one on which it is developed, sound, still images, and motion images should be tested for compatibility. Motion images can be a special problem because their effectiveness often depends upon the speed of the delivery computer.

4. Field test the program.

>   Several people should work through the completed program. Hypermedia programs allow individualized branching, so one person might discover a flaw that others bypassed. User options that seemed perfectly sensible to the design team might turn out to be less obvious to some users.

5. Create a viewer version.

>   Most commercial hypermedia packages incorporate a viewer (or runtime) program that can be distributed freely with the developed program. The viewer allows the developed program to be viewed, but it does not permit any changes to be made.

Summary: Presentation Software and Hypermedia Software

Presentation software is commonly used for electronic "slide shows" presented to groups in structured settings. In general, presentation software is easy to use and has a wide variety of special effects available for slide transitions.

Hypermedia software is used for presentations or training that is to be delivered to individuals. Hypermedia software can control a variety of media, incorporates the ability to create branching programs, and often includes a scripting language that allows programmers to create complex commands. These added options make hypermedia training programs more difficult to develop than presentation programs.

Recently, there has been a blurring of the distinctions between these two classes of software. Some of the newer versions of presentation software allow simple branching, while some of the newer hypermedia products have a simple presentation mode that bypasses many of the more complex options. Figure 8.1 contrasts some of the common features of presentation and hypermedia software.

Authoring Systems

Authoring systems such as Authorware by Macromedia, IconAuthor by AimTech Corp., and TenCORE by Computer Teaching Company have evolved as software tools to facilitate the design, development, delivery, and management of computer-based training programs. The most unique aspect of an authoring system is the management component of the software. A typical authoring system not only enables the creation of multimedia-based training materials, but it provides a system to manage the delivery of the training. The management component of a typical authoring system usually includes different levels of access and record-keeping features.

Different levels of access. An authoring system categorizes users and assigns them levels of access. Each category, such as system operators,

	Presentation Software	Hypermedia Software
Platform	DOS, MS Windows, Macintosh	DOS, MS Windows, Macintosh
Outliner	Yes	No
Templates	Yes	Limited
Slide Sorter	Yes	No
Spell Checker	Yes	No
Script Language	No	Yes
Buttons	Limited	Yes
Transitions	Yes	Limited
Sound	Limited	Yes
Video	Limited	Yes
Animation	Limited	Yes
Handouts	Yes	Limited
Slides	Yes	No
Runtime	Yes	Yes
Royalty-Free Presentation	Yes	Varies

Fig. 8.1. Characteristics of presentation and hypermedia software.

administrators, teachers, or students, has a different level of access. For example, a system operator has the maximum amount of control and has the ability to set system characteristics such as display mode, multimedia device connections, and passwords. Students, on the other hand, can only access lessons that are listed on their individual menus.

Record-keeping features. An authoring system creates databases of information on student progress. The recorded data can be used to prompt a student to complete an unfinished lesson, or it can require the student to demonstrate competency in a certain lesson before advancing. Authoring systems can also provide reports ranging from class rosters to item analyses of test questions.

Authoring systems are often categorized by the dominant method used to create lessons. The early systems were variations of popular programming languages and have become known as script-based systems. As graphic user interfaces (GUIs) have improved on desktop workstations, authoring systems have capitalized upon the simplicity of icon-based approaches. Each type has its unique characteristics.

Script-based authoring systems. Script-based systems use lines of computer code to build lessons. Although script-based systems may seem out of touch with the graphic user interfaces available today, there are certain situations where these systems are preferred. A script-based system in the hands of an experienced programmer is one of the fastest ways to create complex programs. Scripting allows almost unlimited control over external devices, databases, LANs, and other external interfaces. Because scripting is such a powerful technique for solving complex training problems, almost all other types of authoring systems include scripting subsets to be used in situations that require sophisticated structures.

Menu-based authoring systems. Lessons are created in a menu-based authoring system by selecting choices listed on the screen. In a simple system, there may be only a few choices available. For example, it might be possible to create information screens, question screens, or feedback screens using a menu-based authoring system, but combining information and a question on the same screen would require script commands. Menu-based systems are generally easy to use, but are limited in flexibility.

Icon-based authoring systems. Icon-based authoring systems are currently the most popular authoring systems. They capitalize on the structure and familiarity of the GUIs that are in common use today. Icon-based systems use small symbols, or icons, to represent the actions that need to be written into the lessons, such as information screens, media events, or question and branching processes. After the icons have been connected into a visual representation of the structure of the lesson, text, pictures, and sounds can be added.

Summary: Authoring Systems

Authoring systems are similar to hypermedia software in a number of ways. Both kinds of software are designed to facilitate the production of multimedia-based, individualized programs. Both often use scripting languages to facilitate complex operations, and both incorporate viewer (sometimes called runtime) packages to deliver the finished programs. Authoring systems, however, have an added component that addresses the management of computer-based training. In addition, the basic price for an authoring system is often 10 times the price of a typical hypermedia program. Finally, license agreements may be more restrictive for authoring systems. A number of authoring systems charge a fee for every workstation used to deliver any program created through the system.

Expert Systems

An expert system is a computer program that models the thought processes of a human. For example, a military mechanic might need to perform a particular complex diagnostic procedure only once or twice a year. Under ordinary circumstances, the mechanic would consult with an expert who has experience with the procedure. If there is no expert available, the mechanic will probably consult technical manuals to identify the correct steps to the procedure. In some cases, it could take a day or more just to locate the needed information. If an expert system model were constructed based on the human expert, this model could be distributed to all mechanics who might face the same problem. When the need arises, the expert system on the computer could be used to provide advice on the proper steps to follow to solve the problem.

Structure of Expert Systems

While there are several basic expert systems structures, the rule-based system (RBS) is of particular interest because it functions well in applications that emulate human experts or advisors. An RBS is made up of two key components: a *knowledge base* and an *inference engine*. The knowledge base consists of rules and facts that a human expert has defined as essential elements for solving a particular problem. The inference engine is a program that keeps track of what is and what is not known about a problem, and it uses logic to determine what to do next to solve the problem.

Knowledge bases and inference engines can be created from practically any programming language, but many hours of work are required. A number of companies have introduced software packages, called expert system shells, that minimize the effort required to create a customized expert system. An expert system shell contains an inference engine and a simplified method for creating a knowledge base.

In a way, the expert system shell does for expert systems what authoring systems do for computer-based instruction. By using a shell, one can concentrate on the details of the knowledge base without having to write complex programs for an inference engine and knowledge base.

Selecting an Expert System Shell

There are at least a dozen commercial expert system shells available for microcomputers. Selection of a system depends upon a number of factors (See figure 8.2 on page 148). The shell should be matched to the preferences of the programmer for menu-based or command-line programming. Also, shells handle graphics, mouse inputs, and animations with varying degrees of success.

An important issue to consider when purchasing expert system shells relates to the licensing for use of a finished product. Some shells require all users of an expert system that is created on that shell to purchase the entire software package just to use the expert system. Other shell packages offer a runtime package to run finished shells, but it must be purchased separately. Finally, a few expert system shells allow an individual to distribute a runtime version of an expert system for no additional charge. As expert system shell programs grow into a more competitive market, the free runtime license policy may become more common.

Product Name	Platform	Features	Price Range
EXSYS	DOS, Windows, VAX/VMS, UNIX, and OS2 formats	If-Then-Else Rule based Links to databases and spreadsheets	$1,500 (Windows version) $175 Student version
KBMS	Windows, UNIX, mainframes	Uses rules, pattern matching, natural language	$8,500
LEVEL 5-OBJECT	Windows, development and delivery; UNIX, VAX, delivery only	Object-oriented, multimedia, links to many databases	$1,000
VP-EXPERT	DOS	Rule-based, forward and backward chaining, database access, hypertext	$350

Fig. 8.2. Examples of several expert system shells with approximate costs.

Intelligent Tutoring Systems

An ideal intelligent tutoring system (ITS) would be composed of computer modules that accurately model the major components of the teaching/learning environment. One module would contain the subject matter content. Sometimes called the *domain* module, this component would resemble an expert system and contain all relevant information about the topic. The domain module would be designed to be interchangeable so that subject matter content could be upgraded without having an impact on the rest of the system.

A second module in an ideal intelligent tutoring system would focus on the student. This module would keep records of individual student preferences and progress. These systems would learn from students, so that if a student discovers a previously undefined method for solving a problem, the system would validate it and store it for future use.

Another module would contain the teacher, or instructional component. It would include information on learner assessment, instructional strategies, feedback techniques, discipline, and other things that make a "good" teacher. Instructional design would also be an important component of the teacher module. The standard techniques of analysis, design, development, implementation, and evaluation would be blended in with activities such as media selection.

The ideal ITS would work something like this: A student would sit at a workstation and log in. If the ITS recognized the student as a regular, it would start up where the last lesson left off, unless the student requested something different. If the student was new to the system, the tutor would check its databases to see if test scores or prior records had been stored. If not, the tutor would begin a process of familiarization that might include the determination of basic entry skills, preferred learning styles, and so forth.

Once an ITS was working with a student, it would function in much the same way as a talented human tutor would function. Although there might be a preferred path of instruction, the tutor would not blindly follow it. If a student was having trouble with a concept, the tutor would not continue to respond with, "Sorry, try again." Instead, it might try a whole new approach to the problem.

Intelligent tutoring systems exist in experimental and prototype forms, but most do not incorporate all of the components of an ideal system. The basic problem facing developers of ITS software is the underlying lack of understanding of what exactly leads to successful human learning. We do not fully understand how people learn, and we do not fully understand what makes a "good" teacher. Without such understanding, it is impossible to construct accurate models of these processes.

Performance Support Systems

We have recently witnessed a major change in the way corporate and industrial workers are trained. The vast majority of employees now have ready access to computers, and their "in" and "out" boxes are electronic. Employees no longer have to go down the hall to the computer lab to complete a computer-based training (CBT) tutorial—they have a computer right on their desks, and it may be networked to all the other computers. Along with this shift in hardware availability, more powerful software programs have evolved—one of which is electronic Performance Support Systems (PSS).

Electronic Performance Support Systems are designed to provide information, training, and resources to users "on-demand." The possible categories within a PSS include reference databases, advice, online help, computer applications, productivity software, and training

A PSS differs from CBT in many ways. With CBT, the training is often available only by appointment in the computer lab or similar facility. In addition, CBT courses are usually conducted prior to a person's need. For example, an employee may attend a CBT session on how to use spreadsheets in anticipation of new job responsibilities. A problem with this approach is that, by the time the employee needs the new skill, a large percentage of the knowledge and skill may be lost on the "forgetting curve." The training component of a PSS, however, is integrated into the employee's desktop system, along with the spreadsheets, databases, applications, and so on. With a PSS, the training is available when the learner needs it, reducing the problems of retention between training and application.

Another difference between a CBT program and a PSS is the structure. CBT lessons are structured hierarchically. Either the program branches the learners based on their performances, or students navigate through a series of menus to access the lesson they want. In each case, routes between lesson components are limited. The structure of a PSS, however, is built on multiple access routes and hyperlinks to other components of the system. This design permits flexible navigation and information access by users in a nonlinear fashion. Students can access context-sensitive training from their desktops and can easily navigate between PSS components (i.e., from a spreadsheet to online help to training).

Another difference between CBT and a PSS training program is the amount of student monitoring available. With CBT, student activity and performance on questions and exercises is tracked. This tracking, however, is independent of personnel files and system records. Because a PSS is more closely related to total employee support, the training component of a PSS can be monitored and tracked from the system level. The integration of the training component with the system allows context-sensitive advice, information, control, and various types of support.

Most of the current PSS systems are custom-designed products. For example, Analysis & Technology, Inc., has developed a PSS for maintenance technicians. With this system, the technicians can access technical documentation, training on maintenance procedures, and illustrated parts break-down (IPB) information. The IPB component contains engineering drawings of each assembly (See fig. 8.3). Users can manipulate the drawings and zoom the view in or out. The PSS also links to a database containing all of the textual IPB information (Government Standards, vendor, part numbers, descriptions, and attaching parts).

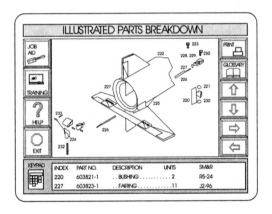

Fig. 8.3. Illustrated parts breakdown component of PSS.

Many experts in the field are confident that performance support systems that can embed training into employee workstations represent the future of computer-based training. As microcomputers become more powerful and operating systems evolve into concurrent processing systems, PSSs might soon show up as commercial products. In any event, this is one area that all training professionals should track very closely.

Group Decision Support Systems

The software products that have been covered so far in this chapter focus upon the development and delivery of information or training. In addition to these tools, instructional developers use a variety of database managers, spreadsheets, word processors, and other assorted professional productivity tools. It is beyond the scope of this text to provide details on all of the productivity tools; however, there is an evolving class of software, called group decision support system software, that is worthy of discussion.

Group decision support system (GDSS) software does exactly what its name suggests—it helps people make decisions. In particular, it helps groups of people reach consensus on complex issues. This is a new category of software that has not yet developed a defined vocabulary, and it is also called group consensus software, group decisionware, or groupware.

In a typical decision-making session, a problem is identified and some preliminary ideas are suggested. Participants gather at their respective workstations (perhaps in a large room with LAN terminals, or perhaps at remote areas connected through telecommunications), review the ideas, and react to them. At appropriate points along the way, the facilitator calls certain topics for a vote, and the participants enter their votes through the computers. A chart—immediately displayed on the computer screen—shows the results of the voting. Discussions and voting continue until consensus is reached. When this happens, the facilitator will confirm the solution and send summary files to all participants.

While this new form of software is still in its infancy, it will almost certainly change the way people in business conduct meetings. Companies that continue to spend several days to transport key personnel to central locations for open-ended meetings will find that they have lost the competitive edge.

Conclusion

The software used in instructional settings has grown remarkably over the last 10 years. Then, almost all instructional programs were highly linear and text-based. Now, many new instructional programs adapt to meet the needs of the individual and include multimedia content. To a great extent, these advances are possible because sophisticated new development programs enable instructional designers to use the multimedia hardware that has become common in desktop workstations.

Development Resources

Presentation Software

Aldus Corp. (Persuasion), 411 First Avenue S., Seattle, WA 98104, 206-622-5500

Alpha Software Corp. (Bravo!), 168 Middlesex Turnpike, Burlington, MA 01803, 800-451-1018

Asymetrix Corp. (Compel), 110 110th Avenue NE, #700, Bellevue, WA 98004, 800-448-6543

Claris (Claris Impact), Claris Corporation, 5201 Patrick Henry Drive, Santa Clara, CA 95052, 800-544-8554

Computer Associates (CA-Cricket Presents), One Computer Associates, Islandia, NY 11788, 800-225-5224

Lotus Development Corp. (Freelance Graphics for Windows), 55 Cambridge Parkway, Cambridge, MA 02142, 800-343-5414

Macromedia Inc. (Action!), 600 Townsend Street, San Francisco, CA 94103, 800-288-4797

Microsoft Corp. (PowerPoint), One Microsoft Way, Redmond, WA 98052, 800-426-9400

Motion Works (ADDmotion II PROmotion), 1020 Mainland Street, Vancouver BC, V6B 2T4, 604-685-9975

Gold Disk, Inc. (Astound), P.O. Box 789, Streetsville, Mississauga, ON L5M 2C2, Canada, 905-602-0395

Software Publishing Corp. (Harvard Graphics for Windows), P.O. Box 4772, Crawfordsville, IN 47933, 800-234-2500

WordPerfect Corp. (Presentations), 1555 N. Technology Way, Orem, UT 84057, 800-451-5151

Soft Craft (Presenter 2), 26 N. Carroll Street, Madison, WI 53703, 608-257-3300

The Zuma Group (Curtain Call), 6733 N. Black Canyon Highway, Phoenix, AZ 85015, 800-332-3492

Hypermedia Software

Allegiant Technologies, Inc. (SuperCard), 6496 Weathers Place, San Diego, CA 92121, 619-587-0500

Apple Computer (HyperCard), One Infinite Loop, Cupertino, CA 95014, 408-996-1010

Ask Me Multimedia (Ask Me), 7100 Northland Circle, Minneapolis, MN 55428, 612-531-0603

Asymetrix Corporation (Multimedia ToolBook), 110 110th Avenue NE, Bellevue, WA 98004, 800-624-8999

IBM Corporation (LinkWay Live!), Old Orchard Road, Armonk, NY 10504, 800-426-3333

Mathematica (Tempra), P.O. Box 105, Westtown, PA 19395, 800-852-6284

Roger Wagner Publishing (HyperStudio), 1050 Pioneer Way, El Cajon, CA 92020, 800-421-6526

Spinnaker Software (Spinnaker Plus), 201 Broadway, Cambridge, MA 02139, 800-323-8088

Vividus (Cinemation), 378 Cambridge Avenue, Palo Alto, CA 94015, 415-321-2221

Authoring Software

AimTech Corp. (IconAuthor), 20 Trafalgar Square, Nashua, NH 03063-1973, 800-289-2884

Allen Communication, Inc. (Quest), 5225 Wiley Post Way, Salt Lake City, UT 84116, 800-325-7850

American Training International (TourGuide), 12638 Beatrice Street, Los Angeles, CA 90066, 800-955-5284

Computer Teaching Corp. (TenCore), 1713 S. State, Champaign, IL 61820, 217-352-6363

Discovery Systems International (Course Builder), 7325 Oak Ridge Highway, Suite 100, Knoxville, TN 37931, 615-690-8829

Global Information Systems Technology, Inc. (TIE Authoring System), 100 Trade Centre Drive, Ste. 301, Champaign, IL 61820, 800-327-0565

InfoAccess, Inc. (Guide), 2800 156th Avenue, SE, Bellevue, WA 98007, 800-344-9737

Interactive Image Technologies (Authority), 908 Niagara Falls Boulevard, North Tonawanda, NY 14120, 800-263-5552

Macromedia, Inc. (Authorware Professional), 600 Townsend Street, San Francisco, CA 94103, 800-288-4797

Pinnacle Courseware, Inc. (Saber Authoring System), 4340 Stevens Creek Boulevard, San Jose, CA 95129, 408-249-8383

Technology Applications Group, Inc. (Sam), 675 E. Big Beaver Road, Troy, MI 48083, 800-659-5214

Expert System Shells

Acquired Intelligence, Inc. (Acquire), 1095 McKenzie Avenue, Victoria, BC, Canada V8P 2L5, 604-479-8646

Albathion Software, Inc. (Entrypaq Professional for Windows), 4372 24th Street, San Francisco, CA 94114, 800-338-0364

Exsys, Inc. (Exsys), 1720 Louisiana Boulevard, Albuquerque, NM 87110, 505-256-8356

ICARUS Corp. (Mentor), 11300 Rockville Pike, One Central Plaza, Rockville, MD 20852, 3018819350

Information Builders, Inc. (Level V Object), 1250 Broadway, New York, NY 10001, 800-444-4303

Instant Recall, Inc. (Tailor), P.O. Box 42294, Washington, DC 20015, 202-966-2582

KDS Corp. (KDS3), 934 Cornell Street, Wilmette, IL 60091, 708-251-2621

Knowledge Garden, Inc. (Micro Expert), Stony Brook Technology Park, 12-8 Technology Drive, Setauket, NY 11733, 516-246-5400

Trinzic Corp.(KBMS for Windows), One Harbor Place, Ste. 500, Portsmouth, NH 03801-3872, 603-427-0444

WordTech Systems Inc. (VP-Expert), 21 Altarinda Road, Orinda, CA 94563, 510-254-0900

Group Decision Support Software

Collaborative Technologies Corp. (VisionQuest), 3373 Towerwood Drive, Dallas, TX 75234, 800-856-6338

Eden Systems Corp. (The Meeting Room), 9302 N. Meridan Street, Indianapolis, IN 46260, 800-779-6338

Ventana Corp. (GroupSystems V), 1430 E. Fort Lowell Road, #301, Tucson, AZ 85719, 800-368-6338

Recommended Reading

Aiken, M. 1993. Using a group decision support system as an instructional aid and exploratory study. *International Journal of Instructional Media* 19(4): 321-28.

Ayre, R., and B. Gottesman. 1994. Group enabled workgroup computing. *PC Magazine* 13(11): 171(9).

Brody, A. 1989. Product comparison: The experts. *Infoworld* (June 19): 59-75.

Burger, J. 1994. New directions in authoring. *NewMedia* 4(5): 45-50.

———. 1994. Presentations step by step. *NewMedia* 4(4): 93-97.

Carr, Clay. 1992. Performance support systems—the next step? *Performance & Instruction* (February): 23-26.

Chapnick, P. 1993. Expert systems catalog of applications. *AI Expert* 8(12): 41(3).

———. 1993. Expert systems in business real world applications. *AI Expert* 8(12): 41(3).

Clark, R. C. 1992. EPSS—Look before you leap: Some cautions about applications of electronic performance support systems. *Performance & Instruction* (May/June): 22-25.

Damore, K. 1993. Beta users praise GRASP for its scripting language: Multimedia program uses flow-chart system. *InfoWorld* 15(3): 19(1).

DeVoney, C. 1993. Multimedia authoring tools: sound, video, interaction. *Windows Sources* 1(5): 360(17).

Enrado, P. 1991. Expert systems resource guide. *AI Expert* 6(5): 52-59.

Fairweather, P. 1992. A model for computer-based training. *AI Expert* 7(12): 30(6).

Gery, G. J. 1991. *Electronic performance support systems.* Boston, Weingarten Press.

Harmon, P., R. Maus, and W. Morrissey. 1988. *Expert systems: Tools and applications,* New York: Wiley & Sons, 68-156.

Helton, T. 1990. Object oriented 5th-generation tool: LEVEL5 OBJECT. *AI Expert* (November): 61-63.

Kranz, M., and V. Sessa. 1994. Meeting makeovers. *PC Magazine* 13(11): 205(6).

LaPlante, A. 1993. '90s style brainstorming. *Forbes* 152(10): 844.

Long, B. 1993. Authorware writes the book on interactivity. *MacWEEK* 7(29): 43(4).

Martinez, C. 1994. All that jazz multimedia authoring software. *Presentations* 8(6): 44(5).

Miller, M. 1944. The changing office. *PC Magazine* 13(11): 112(8).

Murie, M. 1994. Apple breathes new life into HyperCard. *NewMedia.* 4(5): 79-82.

Newquist, H. 1994. Learning the basics. *AI Expert* 9(1): 38(2).

Park, W. 1994. Future trends in authoring. *NewMedia* 4(5): 52-54.

Picarillo, L. 1992. IconAuthor presentation system migrating to Mac. *MacWEEK* 6(43): 14.

Press, L. 1988. Eight-product wrap-up: PC shells. *AI Expert* (September): 61-65.

Ragusa, J., and G. Orwig. 1991. Attacking the information access problem with expert systems. *Journal of Expert Systems* 4: 26-32.

―――. 1990. Expert systems and imaging: NASA's start-up work in intelligent image management. *Journal of Expert Systems* 3: 25-30.

Robinson, P. 1993. Authoring software. *NewMedia 1994 Multimedia Tool Guide* (November): 19-23.

―――. 1993. Presentation and animation software. *NewMedia 1994 Multimedia Tool Guide.* (November): 11-16.

Robinson, P., and L. Lee. 1994. Where presentations meet authoring. *NewMedia* 4(5): 64-67.

Rosenthal, S. 1994. Authorware Pro & IconAuthor the map becomes the territory. *NewMedia* 4(1): 86-90.

―――. 1992. Author! Author! *Publish* 7(9): 54(4).

Ruth, C., and S. Ruth. 1988. *Developing Expert Systems Using 1st-CLASS.* Santa Cruz, CA: Mitchell Publishing.

Schmuller, J., and Y. Mi. 1990. Expert systems shells at work: AI Corporation's 1st-CLASS. *PC AI* (Sept/Oct): 49-53.

―――. 1990. Expert systems shells at work: LEVEL5 OBJECT. *PC AI* (Mar/Apr): 38-40.

Schorr, J. 1993. First time authoring. *MacWorld* 10(3): 106(8).

Shafer, D. 1988. VP-Expert 2.0. *PC AI* (Sept/Oct): 54-60.

Sprague, K. G., and S. R. Ruth. 1988. *Developing expert systems using EXSYS.* Santa Cruz, CA: Mitchell Publishing.

Stylianou, A., G. Madey, and R. Smith. 1992. Selection criteria for expert system shells a socio-technical framework. *Communications of the ACM* 35(10): 30(19).

Toy, D. 1991. Third annual AI product guide. *PC AI* (July/August): 57-62.

Tuck, L. 1994. Presentation software offers power and flexibility. *Presentations* 8(2): 42(4).

Varnadoe, S., and A. E. Barron. 1993. Designing electronic performance support systems. *Journal of Interactive Instruction Development* 6(3): 12-17.

West, N. 1993. Multimedia masters. *MacWorld* 10(3): 114(4).

Wulfekuhle, N. 1994. Selecting a hypermedia authoring program for CBT. *T.H.E. Journal* 21(7): 77(4).

SIMULATIONS AND VIRTUAL REALITY

A Scenario

Eric was flying low and fast over the desert terrain. What had started out as a complex nighttime solo "hit and run" air strike mission had suddenly become even more difficult. He had been ordered to fly at supersonic speeds over the desert to blast an enemy ground-to-air missile site. Now his global navigation system had suddenly gone out. He would have to rely on his own navigational abilities.

The missile site was located in the last of eight valleys formed by a series of huge sand ridges. Eric was flying well south of the site and was supposed to make a sharp turn up the valley immediately parallel to the site. At just the right instant, he was to hop over the ridge, release his armament, and get out fast.

The plane was already passing the third ridge, so Eric decided to keep counting and to trust his own flying skills. Four... five... six... seven, hard bank to the right. He was flying below the ridge, out of reach of the missiles on the other side. He knew that in two minutes his instruments would see the radomes of the site at the top of the ridge ahead and to his left. He was to release two radar-seeking missiles the instant his instrumentation locked on, then cut across the ridge just in front of the domes to release his air-to-ground missiles at the site. If all went well, the enemy would know he was coming, but they might be unable to use their missiles against him.

Suddenly, a warning signal was buzzing loud in Eric's ears. Radar had locked onto him, and his radar-seeking missiles were following those signals back to their origin. But something was wrong. The missiles were tracking a target on the ridge to his right. In the split second that it took him to realize his mistake, Eric saw the first flash of a missile launch directly ahead of him. Within seconds, he saw two more flashes.

Eric had somehow missed a ridge and turned directly up the valley in which the missile site was located. He quickly targeted and launched his air-to-ground missiles at the enemy site, but he was in real trouble now. Even though the enemy radar tracking would be destroyed in an instant, he had less than a minute left to deal with the three missiles that were already launched. One or two missiles might be fooled once they lost radar guidance, but he knew that with three missiles, all of his defensive moves would be anticipated.

In one sharp, dizzying move, he flipped over the ridge to his right and dove into the next valley. Two missiles followed. One hit the ridge, but the other was only seconds from impact. He pulled back hard on the stick and felt the g-suit press against his legs and body as he rocketed up into a perfect arc. There was no sense going in to meet the missile; he preferred to gain a few seconds by making it chase him. At maximum g force, Eric rolled over much higher and in the opposite direction that he had just a moment before. He now had 12 seconds to impact, and he activated the close-range defensive electronics in his plane. Either the missile's electronics had been improved, or it just made a lucky guess out of the mass of conflicting information his defense system was creating, because it kept approaching.

Eric knew his time was up. He grabbed the ejection triggers and pulled hard. There was a terrific blast, then everything became very calm. Soon, the lights came up and a voice over the communication system asked if he wanted to try the same scenario again.

Eric was covered with sweat. He climbed out of the simulator cockpit and hobbled down the stairs to the floor below. Although he was frustrated by the mistake he had made, he decided it was better to make it here in the simulator than in the air. He asked the training team to store his flight and give him a couple of minutes to recover before he reviewed it.

* * * *

Introduction

The technology described in the scenario is not fictional. Simulations and virtual reality have become common topics of discussion in training environments. Military organizations in many countries now use advanced simulations for mission training. While such realistic simulations are still very complex and expensive, simulations, simulators, and virtual reality are rapidly filtering into business and industry training. This chapter will:

- Clarify the differences among simulations, simulators, and virtual reality.
- Describe the characteristics of a simulation.
- Provide examples of simulations with training components.

- Describe the characteristics of a virtual reality program.
- Provide examples of virtual reality applications with training components.
- Provide sources for additional information.

Simulations, simulators, and virtual reality are closely related terms. A simulation is a representation of an event for which real, hands-on training might be too dangerous, expensive, complex, or time-consuming. Simulations include board games such as Monopoly, role-playing exercises, and airplane flight programs on computers. The simulation is the set of rules or algorithms that describes and models a real-life event. Most current discussions of simulations in training involve computers.

A simulator is the device or medium that delivers a simulation. The simulator might be a game board with playing pieces, a group seminar setting, a computer, or a machine connected to one or more computers. A simulator alone is about as useful as an empty videotape player. The model of the real-life event, the simulation, makes the simulator function.

The terms *simulation* and *simulator* are often used as synonyms. For example, a popular software package for microcomputers is titled *Microsoft Flight Simulator*. This software is really a simulation; only when the program is loaded into an appropriate computer with a good color display and a set of flight controls (a steering yoke or joystick and foot pedals) does the entire system become a flight simulator.

Few experts agree on precisely what constitutes *virtual reality* (VR). Most, however, agree that a virtual reality application is an advanced form of simulation. In a typical virtual reality application, the participant becomes an active player. A special helmet might provide three-dimensional views of the setting, and electronic gloves might provide tactile input and feedback. In such a case, the participant might view an electronic representation of his or her hand through the display in the helmet. The virtual hand moves in unison with the participant's biological hand and is capable of manipulating electronic objects that are visible through the helmet. For example, the participant might locate, pick up, and toss a virtual ball. In advanced systems, the computer might even use electronics in the glove to provide feedback that creates sensations of the hardness and weight of the ball.

Simulations

A simulation is a model of an object or event. With a flight simulator, the simulation must model an aircraft and all of its flight characteristics. The more accurate the model, the more realistic the flight simulation. The laws of physics (aerodynamics in particular) are used to create basic formulas that describe airflow around the surfaces of the chosen aircraft, vectors, and flight characteristics. Additional formulas describe the craft itself in terms of shape, weight, power, control surfaces, and so on.

All of these formulas are then combined into a program and fed into a computer. The program for a flight simulator is designed to be cyclical. In other words, as soon as all calculations are completed, they start over again, including any new values from the previous pass through the calculations. For example, if the simulated aircraft were flying "straight and level" at a constant velocity, very few new values would be generated. However, if the aircraft power were suddenly increased in the simulation, each pass through the calculations would produce new values for speed, lift, torque, and other critical variables as the aircraft accelerated. Because many of these variables interrelate, each pass through the calculations must use fresh information from the previous pass.

Cycle Time

The amount of time it takes a computer to make one complete pass through the calculations of a continuous simulation is called the *cycle time*. In an aircraft simulation, a cycle time of one or two seconds would be too slow because it would create an unrealistic jerky representation of the airplane and the forces that control it. A cycle time of 30 or 40 per second would create a much more realistic simulation. Cycle time is an important factor in many simulations; one common solution to a slow cycle time is to use a more powerful computer.

Terrain Models

Even the most sophisticated flight simulation model would not be very useful if all it displayed were the aircraft instruments. Most pilots rely upon external visual cues for flight, and a terrain model must be created to provide the visual inputs. A terrain model is really a simulation within a simulation. It is a series of formulas that create a dynamic visual display of some real or imaginary portion of the earth. When the terrain model is given precise coordinates and orientation (looking up, down, at an angle, etc.), it creates a view of how the terrain would look from that perspective. In a flight simulation, the model of the aircraft calculates the coordinates of the aircraft at the end of each cycle and feeds that information to the terrain model. The terrain model then creates a view out of the cockpit window that represents those coordinates.

The terrain model also sends information back to the simulation. For example, if the terrain model signaled that the coordinates of the aircraft matched the coordinates of a tall building, a "crash" would be indicated and the simulation would end.

Simulators

Both the aircraft simulation and the terrain model would be of little use without a means for human interaction. This interaction is provided through the simulator. A flight simulator can be simple, a basic personal computer with a joystick for aircraft control and a standard computer monitor to display the terrain model. While such simulators can provide entertainment and basic levels of training, they do not come close to representing the real "feel" of an airplane in flight.

A more complex flight simulator might be a model of a real cockpit, where all controls and instruments are designed to function as they would in the airplane. This cockpit is attached to a mechanical system that moves it into all possible attitudes. Finally, a complex display system would project forward and side views of the terrain onto screens that surround the cockpit.

To maximize realism, many flight simulations insert "intelligent life" into the terrain. In a passenger aircraft simulation, air traffic controllers, other aircraft, storms, and malfunctions are common features. In a military flight simulation, enemy aircraft, friendly aircraft, weapons systems, and enemy defensive systems are all part of the terrain. These interactions increase the realism of the training that is delivered through the simulation and simulator.

Types of Simulations

The aircraft model provides a good example of the typical components of a simulation/simulator system; however, not all simulations represent aircraft, and not all simulators are complex mechanical devices that provide a variety of motion effects. According to Alessi and Trollip (1991, 119), simulations that are used for education and training fall into four general classes: physical, process, procedural, and situational.

Physical Simulations

Physical simulations focus on the representations of physical objects, and they are among the most common simulations used for training. Possible training topics include the study of ballistics through simulated cannons and projectiles, the operation of an internal combustion engine, or the operation of a SONAR console.

Process Simulations

Alessi and Trollip (1991) identify process simulations as those that are designed to teach about an intangible concept. Often the simulation is either accelerated or slowed from real time in order to allow the learner to more clearly understand the concept. For example, a simulated genetics experiment on fruit flies can be understood more clearly when many generations of fruit flies are studied. In such a simulation, certain characteristics of parent fruit flies are chosen, then the results are followed through many generations of offspring. The life cycle of the fruit flies is greatly accelerated so that these results can be observed within minutes instead of months or years.

Procedural Simulations

Procedural simulations teach a sequence of actions or series of steps needed to accomplish a task. Some procedural simulations focus on cognitive, or thinking, skills, while others relate more to psychomotor, or physical coordination, skills. For example, a cognitive simulation might enable the learner to practice medical diagnostics on an emergency room patient. The simulation would start by describing some of the basic medical characteristics of the patient, and the learner would respond by requesting actions and tests that would help to identify the problem. On the other hand, a psychomotor procedural simulation might enable a learner to develop the coordination skills required to use a robotic arm control for the handling of radioactive materials.

Situational Simulations

Alessi and Trollip (1991, 127) identify situational simulations as programs that deal more with "the attitudes and behaviors of people." Role playing simulations fit this category. For example, a multimedia simulation might show a suicidal patient dashing into a psychologist's office. Depending upon the learner's interactions with the patient, he or she either calms down enough to accept help from the psychologist or jumps out the 10th floor window.

Role playing simulations are beneficial in many professions because it is too risky to practice on real people. Until recently, carefully trained live actors were used as the patients, but this has been prohibitively expensive. Now, many alternative scenes are prepared on videodisc, and a computer controls the interactions.

Training Applications of Simulations

Almost all simulations can be used to help people learn, although some simulations do not have specific training components built into them. For example, meteorologists learn about weather prediction by trying to build an accurate simulation of global weather. This is an effective learning tool even though such a simulation does not contain specific training components. Another example of a simulation that lacks a specific training component is an aerodynamic simulator that predicts the amount of air drag produced by a new car design. Because reducing air drag improves gas mileage, almost all new car designs go through simulations before the initial models are built. Over a period of time, engineers learn that several basic shapes, such as the currently popular wedge shape, consistently produce low amounts of air drag.

However, many simulations are designed with specific training components. For example, a flight simulator might collect performance data from a student pilot and then identify the specific maneuvers that need more practice. A cardiopulmonary resuscitation simulator might instruct a learner to press at a slightly different location on the model's chest to minimize the chance of rib injuries.

In general, simulations without specific training components are used in developmental research, or they are used with learners who are refining skills that have already been highly developed. Simulations with training components are often used with novice learners, or with learners who are adapting previously learned skills to a new application.

Virtual Reality

Virtual reality (VR) is a form of advanced simulation. There is no clear division between the most sophisticated simulations and the most basic of virtual reality applications, but many experts agree on several characteristics that identify a virtual reality application. Frequently mentioned characteristics of VR applications are inclusion, manipulation, and navigation.

Inclusion

A true VR application immerses the participant in the virtual world of the application. As technology improves, some of the pioneers in VR are predicting that it will become difficult for participants to differentiate between the real world and virtual worlds.

While current technology is nowhere near this level of sophistication, we are gaining a better understanding of what is needed to create realistic virtual worlds. Vision is among the most important of the senses, and a virtual world supplies participants with high resolution, three-dimensional color views. A person's eyes will focus in the distance for distant objects and more closely for nearby objects. Sounds should be three-dimensional as well. If a sound comes from a source behind the participant, it should swing around to the front as the participant turns around to attend to it.

Manipulation

While many simulations allow participants to manipulate factors that impact the simulation, none approach the level of manipulation anticipated in advanced VR applications. In a virtual world, virtual objects can be manipulated at will. In a VR exercise world, virtual tennis rackets might be used to play a virtual tennis game.

Manipulation has many potential applications in education and training. It is likely that surgeons will be able to practice complex surgical techniques by using imaginary instruments on virtual patients. The complex and expensive aircraft simulators of today might be replaced with virtual simulators. The only tangible object will be the flight seat that the pilot sits in. All control devices, instruments, and sensations of flight will be created through sensory devices embedded in a flight suit and helmet worn by the pilot.

Navigation

Many forms of VR require that the participant be able to navigate through the virtual world. A person may be allowed to "fly" from place to place by simply pointing in the desired direction. In more advanced systems, the participant might stand inside a platform that is designed to allow him or her to "walk" without really going anywhere, somewhat like an exercise treadmill. Navigation is important in VR applications because it allows the participant to gain different perspectives of the virtual environment. For example, a VR system might be used to model a kitchen design for a prospective homeowner. With appropriate VR devices, the customer would be able to walk around the room and manipulate cabinet doors and appliances. He or she could open the dishwasher door and determine whether or not there is still room to get around behind it.

Tools of VR

Virtual reality applications are designed to be aware of the participant. In such applications, the computer constantly collects information on the location and motions of the participant through special gloves, tracking devices, and platforms.

Data Input Gloves

While keyboards, mice, and joysticks can be used to input data into a computer, none of these devices represent the natural ways a human manipulates objects in the real world. The most important advance in input devices for VR is a method of capturing the movements of the hand. This is accomplished with a glove that contains sensors to measure the flexing of fingers, the rotation of the wrist, and the movement of the arm. As a result, the computer can construct a real-time model of the human hand as it moves about in space.

These gloves have been given a common name of data gloves, although the *DataGlove* is a specific product of VPL Research. Data input gloves vary in price and complexity, ranging from $8,000 for the original DataGlove to $15 for used video game accessories. The most expensive gloves measure very fine movements of the fingers and wrist, while less expensive gloves detect only two or three positions for several fingers and do not measure wrist movements at all (See fig. 9.1).

One of the most popular data input gloves for computer hobbyists has been the Power Glove by Mattel. This glove was originally intended to control video games, but it never sold well for this application. Production was discontinued, but many computer hobbyists still browse through flea markets and garage sales in search of used Power Gloves. Books such as *Garage Virtual Reality* (Jacobson 1994) provide details on adapting this glove to microcomputer virtual reality applications.

**Fig. 9.1. Motion sensors
on a typical data input glove.**

Head Mounted Displays

The visual display is the "window" to VR. As one would expect, the better the visual display, the better the realism of the VR application. Although several techniques have been used to create true three-dimensional images on standard computer monitors, these techniques have limited application in the world of VR. One must keep in mind that the concept of VR inclusion mandates that the participant become immersed in the virtual environment. This is difficult to achieve with a standard computer monitor.

Instead, what is needed is a display device that allows the participant to explore the entire virtual environment by simply looking around. If the participant is in a virtual forest, there will be sky and leaves above, grass below, and trees all around. The participant should be able to experience all of these. At the present, there are two display technologies that simulate such experiences. One technique is to provide a large hemispherical room with multiple computer projectors that overlap to provide one huge, enveloping, seamless image. Although the costs are considerable, the level of realism is high.

The second technique is a display headset worn by the participant (See figure 9.2 on page 166). The headset is designed to provide a three-dimensional view that mimics the field of view of normal human vision. As the participant moves, sensors monitor the viewing direction and create appropriate images of the virtual world from that particular view. While these systems are designed to monitor head and body movements, they cannot yet deal with eye movements. As a result, a VR participant looks left by turning left, right by turning right, and up and down in similar manners. Moving only the eyes in some direction does not cause a change in the view.

As you might guess, conflicting signals are sent to the brain when a participant uses a VR headset. There is no reaction to eye movements, and all virtual objects, whether near or far, are really only in focus at one specific distance (the focal setting point of the optics), and there is usually some amount of delay between head movements and the appearance of the new perspective on the screen. Most people comment that this last factor (called lag time) is the most distracting of conflicts. In fact, some people have so much trouble adapting to the delay that they become nauseous.

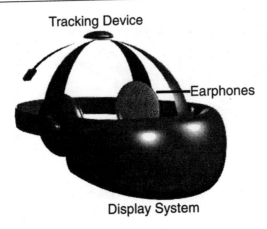

Tracking Device

Earphones

Display System

Fig. 9.2. Components of a head mounted display.

Head Tracking

Headsets are used to create the three-dimensional images in a VR system, but they must also tell the computer where the participant is looking so that the application can create the appropriate scene. Most headsets use magnetic or ultrasonic tracking devices to provide information about the participant looking left, right, up, or down. Some systems can also detect a person tilting his or her head from shoulder to shoulder or even physically moving around within a limited space.

It is the combination of a head mounted display, data glove, and a tracking system that makes VR possible on small computers (See fig. 9.3). It takes an enormous amount of computing power to construct dynamic, three-dimensional images and to track head and hand movements. As microcomputers become more powerful, VR systems will become more common.

Sound Reproduction

Although sound is an important component of most environments, the accurate reproduction of sound in a virtual reality application has turned out to be even more challenging than the reproduction of images. While it is possible to create high fidelity sounds through computers, the challenge applies more to the perceived realism of the sounds. Sounds, even more so than images, are three-dimensional. Even though we cannot see what is behind us, we can hear it, and we can locate it in relation to us.

A true VR system would generate sounds in such a way that they resemble reality. If a sound came from behind a participant, that sound would shift around to the front of the person as he or she turned to face it. Such advanced sound synthesis systems do not yet exist for the microcomputer market. Research is underway, however, and it is likely that in a few years

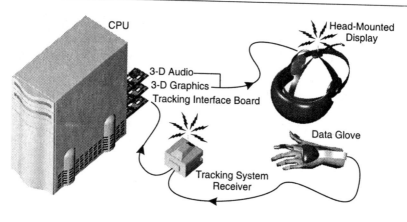

Fig. 9.3. Components of a VR system.

small head mounted displays will present both high resolution, three-dimensional pictures and realistic, three-dimensional sounds.

Navigation Platforms

The final characteristic of virtual reality, navigation, requires some method for allowing the participant to move from place to place within the virtual environment. In most cases, it is not possible to allow a person to simply walk around because cables connect the head mounted display, data gloves, and tracking system to the computer. In addition, real walls and other obstacles would certainly interrupt the participant's virtual experience. As a result, alternatives to real locomotion have been examined. In some cases, the participant simply points in the desired direction of travel, but while this is easy to accomplish through the data glove, it prevents the glove from being used for other activities.

A more promising method of locomotion involves a platform with a variety of sensors. The participant leans against a circular rail around the platform to initiate motion in any particular direction, with the force against the rail determining the speed. Climbing stairs is initiated by raising one foot after the other in a climbing motion. Some platforms are even using devices like treadmills to allow real walking motions.

Training Applications of VR

If the discussion of virtual reality sounds like science fiction, that is because most of the technology is still speculative at this point in time. Current applications of VR are curiosities that have some entertainment value, but most of them are not ready for "prime time" yet. However, this area of technology is developing rapidly, and within a few years, VR will be ready to be applied to the training market.

It is likely that the first effective uses of VR in training will be applications that rely heavily upon navigation. For example, the U.S. Navy is developing a VR program to train naval recruits to move efficiently about an aircraft carrier before they are physically transferred to the ship. This would allow the new recruits to become fully functional more quickly.

Eventually VR will be used for far more sophisticated aspects of training. For example, it is possible that surgeons will practice rare procedures on virtual patients. The imaginary instruments will have the same weight and feel as the real instruments. If this scenario is carried a step further, it might be possible for an experienced surgeon to operate on a real patient who is thousands of miles away. While the real surgeon performs the operation in a virtual world, a robot at the surgical site would be duplicating every microscopic move on the real patient.

Conclusion

Simulations and virtual reality are technologies that have enormous potential for training environments. They enhance the transfer of training because they can provide visual, aural, and tactile realism that are impossible through other technologies. Our increasing knowledge of how human beings receive and process information will help us determine appropriate applications for these advanced techniques.

References

Alessi, S., and S. Trollip. (1991). *Computer based instruction; Methods and development.* 2d ed. Englewood Cliffs, NJ: Prentice-Hall.

Resources

A.R.C. Software (Dance of the Planets), P.O. Box 1955, Loveland, CO 80539, 800-759-1642

Abbot, Foster & Hauserman Co. (Brain Simulator), North 8526 Antietam Court, Spokane, WA 99208, 509-466-8778

The Academic Software Library (Physics Simulation Programs), Box 8202, North Carolina State University, Raleigh, NC 27695, 800-955-8275

AT&T ISTEL Visual Interactive Systems, Inc. (Witness for Windows), 25800 Science Park Drive, Cleveland, OH 44122, 216-292-2668

Autodesk, Inc. (Cyberspace Developers Kit), 2320 Marinship Way, Sausalito, CA 94965, 800-879-4233

Bay Options (Option Simulator), 1235 Walnut Street, Berkeley, CA 94709, 510-845-6425

Biosoft (Cardiolab), P.O. Box 10938, Ferguson, MO 63135, 314-524-8029

CACI Products Co. (SIMSCRIPT II.5), 3333 N. Torrey Pines Court, La Jolla, CA 92037, 619-457-9681

Computer Explorations, Inc. (Cyber View), 9178 Willowbrook, Huntsville, AL 35802, 205-882-9490

Datathon, Inc. (TrainEase), 19360 Rinaldi Street, Northridge, CA 91326, 818-701-9642

Dolphin Marine Systems, Inc. (Sailing Instructor System), 406 Lloyd Avenue, P.O. Box 188, Downingtown, PA 19335, 800-367-3622

Eastman Kodak Co. (Kodak PCphotographer), 343 State Street, Rochester, NY 14650, 800-242-2424

IBM (Tutorial Manager/2), Old Orchard Road, Armonk, NY 10504, 800-426-3333

Knowledge House Publishing Ltd. (Patient Simulator II), 3845 Dutch Village Road, Halifax, Nova Scotia, B3L 4H9, 9024551962

Legent Corp. (Phoenix System), 575 Herndon Parkway, Herndon, VA 22070, 800-676-LGNT

MathWorks, Inc. (SimuLink for Windows), 24 Prime Park Way, Natick, MA 01760, 508-653-1415

Maxis (SimCity), 2 Theater Square, Orinda, CA 94563, 800-336-2947

Mentor Graphics Corp. (Idea Station), 8005 S.W. Boeckman Road, Wilsonville, OR 97070, 800-547-3000

Microsoft Corp. (Microsoft Flight Simulator), One Microsoft Way, Redmond, WA 98052, 800-426-9400

PROMODEL Corp. (ProModel for Windows), 1875 S. State, Orem, UT 84058, 801-226-6036

Sietec Open Systems (Visual Builder for Windows), 1131 A. Leslie Street, Don Mills, Ontario M3C 3L8, 800-565-5650

Sony Electronic Publishing Co. (LawnMower Man), 711 Fifth Avenue, New York, NY 10022, 800-654-8802

Virtual Reality Laboratories, Inc. (Vistapro), 2341 Ganador Court, San Luis Obispo, CA 93401, 800-829-VRLI

VPL Research (DataGlove),Vream, Inc. (Vream Virtual Reality Development System), 2568 N. Clark Street, Chicago, IL 60614, 312-477-0425

Recommended Reading

Barr, C. 1993. Businesses play war games. *PC Magazine* 12(11): 31(1).

Bauer, C. 1993. Future soldiers train on virtual battlefields; Army develops IPort simulator to create realistic combat environments for troops. *Government Computer News* 12(20): 43(2).

Biocca, F. 1992. Virtual reality technology: A tutorial. *Journal of Communication* 42(4): 23(49).

Carlson, P. 1993. SimCity 2000. *MacWEEK* 7(47): 48(1).

Franchi, J. 1994. Virtual reality: An overview. *Tech Trends* 39(1): 23(4).

Gillen, A. 1993. Simulating the future. *MIDRANGE Systems* 6(24): 20(1).

Graves, G. 1993. NASA's virtual reality. *NewMedia* 3(1): 36-41.

Greenfield, R. 1994. Toward a virtual Navy. *NewMedia* 4(4): 33.

Heath, J. 1994. Virtual reality resource guide. *AI Expert* 9(5): 32(14).

Jacobson, L. 1994. *Garage virtual reality.* Indianapolis, IN: Sams Publications.

Knerr, B., et al. 1994. Research in the use of virtual environment technology to train dismounted soldiers. *Journal of Interactive Instruction Development* 6(4): 9-20.

Latta, J. 1994. Virtual reality annual international symposium (VRAIS). *Multimedia Monitor* (February): 14-15.

Louderback, J. 1993. Multimedia fish tank makes case for "Zen-ware." *PC Week* 10(20): 118.

———. 1993. Maxis industry simulation packages don't play games. *PC Week* 10(8): 80.

Mace, S. 1993. Simulator explores health care funding *InfoWorld.* 15(47): 24(1).

Merril, J. 1993. Surgery on the cutting edge: Virtual reality applications in medical education. *Virtual Reality World* (November): 34-38.

Moshell, J. M., B. Blau, L. Xin, and C. Lisle. 1994. Dynamic terrain. *Simulation* 62(1): 29(12).

Neumann, P. 1993. Modeling and simulation. *Communications of the ACM* 36(4): 124.

Nilan, M. 1992. Cognitive space; using virtual reality for large information resource management problems. *Journal of Communication* 42(4): 115(20).

Nilsson, B. 1993. Virtus Walkthrough takes a virtual walk through Windows. *Computer Shopper* 13(12): 869(2).

Reveaux, T. 1993. Virtual reality gets real. *NewMedia* 3(1): 32-35.

Taylor, W. 1993. Virtus's incredible walkthrough: Virtual-reality based drawing. *PCComputing* 6(9): 60.

Temin, T. 1993. DOD trains soldiers with virtual battlefield. *Government Computer News* 12(18): 68(2).

Closing Remarks

Only a few years ago, the hardware for a typical multimedia presentation consisted of up to 24 slide projectors, several dissolve units for transitions, and a program track on a special audio tape player to control the whole show. If all the slides were positioned properly and the program track was prepared accurately, the result was an impressive display of sights and sounds. But things did not always work. Slides would stick and not feed into one of the projectors. Lamps would burn out in the middle of the show. One projector would miss a cue and trail one slide behind. Circuit breakers would trip because multiple projectors required a lot of power. In summary, multimedia presentations used to be very impressive, but troublesome curiosities. They were usually too expensive and inconvenient for a training department. Instead, they were reserved for marketing presentations at conferences.

Multimedia technologies have advanced a great deal in the past few years, and impressive multimedia programs are now within the domain of microcomputers. While multimedia once relied upon hundreds of pounds of equipment and thousands of watts of power to present dazzling shows to crowds at conventions, basic computers with a few inexpensive accessories can now present effective, interactive training for individuals.

However, with progress comes confusion. Complex applications such as digitized motion video are rapidly becoming practical as the processing power of microcomputers continues its constant upward spiral. New applications typically go through a period of rapid growth before they stabilize. During this time, incompatible products often evolve, thrive for a short time, then fade away. At least one product usually follows an upwardly compatible path toward what eventually becomes an industry standard.

There are no accurate ways to see into the future, so there is no fool-proof method to pick the exact multimedia components that will create an eternally "upgradeable" system. So what is a director of a cash-poor training program to do? The best advice is fairly straight forward:

- *Seek practical solutions to practical problems.* Technology is not a cure-all. No matter how many technology-based training dollars you throw at a problem, you will not solve the problem if it is not training-related.

- *Accept depreciation.* A specific technology does not last forever. Neither does training. Accept the fact that technology-based training is no different from more traditional forms of training in that it has a definite shelf life. Make plans to develop training that you can use intensively over a relatively short period, but keep in mind factors that might make future revisions easy. For example, with digital video-based training you should never destroy your original video footage. One of the old out-takes might be exactly what you need for a later revision.

- *Stay informed.* You can do this by reading books and journals, talking with associates, and attending technology conferences and workshops.

Perhaps the last comment is the most important. Many people spend a lot of time and money only to discover something that someone else already knows. By asking questions and learning from others, you will be able to spend far more productive time exploring the exciting potential for multimedia training.

Glossary

10Base2. A standard that defines a thin coaxial cable system, sometimes called "thinnet." This cable is often used in local area networks (LANs).

10Base5. A standard that defines a thick coaxial cable system. This cable is often used in parts of local area networks (LANs) that cover large distances, such as from one building to another.

10BaseT. A standard that defines a twisted pair cable system. This is an inexpensive cable system that is often used in local area networks (LANs) and business telephone systems.

16-bit. A 16-bit video display card can display one of 65,536 different colors for each pixel; a 16-bit audio card stores one of 65,536 values for each sample of sound.

24-bit. A 24-bit video display card can display 16.7 million different colors for each pixel, and it is often referred to as true-color; a 24-bit audio card can store one of 16.7 million values for each sample of sound.

3DO. A compact disc-based technology that was designed to deliver interactive video and audio for entertainment and education in the home market. 3DO is similar (yet incompatible) with CD-i.

8-bit. An 8-bit video display card can display 256 different colors for each pixel; an 8-bit audio card can store one of 256 values for each sample of sound.

Access time. The amount of time required to find and display information from a hard drive, CD-ROM, or other peripheral. Most hard drives now have access times less than 20 milliseconds, while CD-ROM drives have access times between 200 and 700 milliseconds.

ADPCM (Adaptive Delta Pulse Code Modulation). A compression technique usually used for storing digitized sound.

AI. *See* Artificial intelligence.

Algorithm. The set of conditions or equations that define the precise operation of a system. An algorithm might define the compression technique for a digitized image or sound. Or, an algorithm might define the flight characteristics of an airplane. Such an algorithm can then be used to create a simulation of the airplane.

Analog video. Video that is stored as an electrical signal with a continuous scale. Videotape and videodisc generally store analog video.

Analog recording. A method of recording in which the waveform of the recorded signal is stored in a continuous pattern on the storage medium. For videotape, the pattern would be stored as a fluctuating magnetic field.

Archiver. A program that performs compression and decompression on files. Archivers are common in telecommunications because they shrink the size of a file, which makes it possible to download or upload the file faster. The archiver must also be used to decompress the program again before it can be used.

Arcnet. A common network standard, recently standardized, but in use since 1977. Utilizes a token-passing protocol. Common transmission speed is 2.5 megabits per second.

Artificial intelligence. Applications that exhibit human intelligence and behavior. Also implies the ability to learn or adapt through experience.

ASCII (American Standard Code for Information Interchange). A standard that establishes the structure of binary 0s and 1s that define the letters of the alphabet, digits, and common punctuation marks.

Aspect ratio. The width-to-height ratio of an image. Changing the aspect ratio can make images appear out of proportion.

Audio capture. The process of digitizing analog audio signals and storing the resulting data as a file.

Audio teleconferencing. Voice-only communications linking two or more sites. In most cases, standard telephone lines and speakerphones are used.

Audio track. Narration, sounds, and music stored in analog or digital form. Many devices, such as videodiscs have two audio tracks which can be accessed independently or in stereo.

Audiographic teleconferencing. Voice communications supplemented with the transmission of still images. Pictures, graphs, or sketches can be transmitted during the conference. Standard facsimile (fax) machines or computer-driven systems can be used.

Authoring systems. Software that is used to create computer-based training. They contain program components to manage the instructional process.

Bandwidth. The amount of information that a cable or electronic system can transmit at one time. For example, a telephone cable with a narrow bandwidth might be able to handle only one telephone call at a time, while a cable with a wide bandwidth might handle one hundred calls at one time.

Barcode reader. A pen-like wand used to read barcodes from paper. Some barcode readers are connected to the videodisc player with a cable; others use a remote infrared beam.

Barcode. Small parallel lines that can be read and interpreted by a scanner (barcode reader). Barcodes can contain instructions for videodisc players, such as "play from frame 12345 to frame 23876."

Base page. A basic screen of information in a hypermedia program (background color, text fonts, help buttons, etc.) over which all other screens appear. This basic information is created only once, although it shows up on all other screens.

Baseband. Digitally encoded information transmitted in such a way that the entire capacity, or bandwidth, of the cable is utilized.

Baud rate. A term sometimes used to define the speed of serial data transmissions, such as those found with modems. The term is being replaced by bits per second (bps).

BBS. *See* Bulletin board.

Between-frame compression. Video compression that eliminates redundancies that occur from frame to frame. Also referred to as interframe or temporal compression.

Bit (Binary digIT). The smallest unit of information in a digital computer. It is usually represented with values of 0 or 1.

Bit transfer rate. The number of bits transmitted per unit of time. Frequently stated in millions of bits (megabits) per second for LANs.

Bits per second. A common method of measuring the speed of a modem. Modems range in speed from 1,200 bits per second (bps) to 28,800 bps. Modems must be matched to the same bps rate before they can communicate with each other.

Boolean search. The use of logical connectors (and, or, not) to search for a combination of words or phrases.

Brainstorming. A planning process, usually conducted in small groups, that encourages the free flow of ideas.

Branch. A decision point in computer-based training that allows the software to select a route through the training based upon an interaction with the learner.

Bridge. (1) A device, often leased through a telephone company, that links three or more telephone lines together for audio teleconferencing. *See* call-in bridge and call-out bridge. (2) A computer or other device that links two or more local area networks (LANs).

Buffer. *See* Data buffer.

Bulletin board. An electronic bulletin board system (BBS) is a computer-based equivalent of the traditional bulletin board. Most BBS systems also offer an option for private e-mail.

Bus topology. A network in which all workstations are connected to a linear transmission cable.

Button. A specific area of the display screen in a hypermedia program that triggers a predefined action when selected.

Byte. A grouping of eight bits. A byte provides sufficient information to define one ASCII character.

C

Caching programs. Software caching programs use a computer's RAM to save information read from a CD-ROM disc. This procedure helps to speed up the data transfer time.

Caddy. A small plastic case that is required by some CD-ROM drives to hold the compact disc when it is inserted into the drive.

Call-in bridge. A telephone bridge where the conference is established by having all of the distant sites call in to the bridge telephone number. Long-distance charges are billed to the distant locations.

Call-out bridge. A telephone bridge where one location calls all distant sites to connect each site to the teleconference. Any long-distance charges are billed to the one originating location.

Capture. The process of collecting and saving text or image data. For example, most telecommunication programs allow you to save (capture) information to a disk. In a similar manner, many graphics programs allow you to save and manipulate images from other applications.

CAV. *See* Constant angular velocity.

CBT. *See* Computer based training.

CD+G (compact disc plus graphics). Audio compact discs with limited graphics to complement the music.

CD-Audio. *See* Compact Disc Audio.

CD-I. *See* Compact Disc Interactive.

CD-R. *See* Compact Disc Recordable.

CD-ROM XA (Compact Disc-Read Only Memory eXtended Architecture). A CD-ROM format that interleaves the audio with the graphics/text.

CD-ROM. *See* Compact Disc-Read Only Memory.

CGA. *See* Color graphics adapter.

Chapter. One linear segment of a videodisc. Chapter searches can be done through the remote control unit, the barcode reader, or a computer.

Chapter stops. Pre-determined frames on a videodisc that the user can jump to with a remote control, computer, or barcode reader. Most videodiscs have an index of chapter stops listed on the videodisc jacket.

Chat. An option that some telecommunications systems allow which makes it possible for a user to communicate directly with other users. The chatting is not vocal, however; the information typed into each system keyboard is displayed on the other computer(s).

Cinepak. A codec produced by SuperMac for software-only compression. It requires considerable compression time, but results in high quality.

Clip art. Commercial collections of drawings that are licensed for use in other applications.

CLV. *See* Constant linear velocity.

Coaxial cable. A cable made up of one central conductor surrounded by a shielding conductor.

Codec (COder-DECoder or COmpression/DECompression). An electronic device or software program that converts images into compressed data for transmission or storage. The same device can convert compressed data back into viewable signals.

Color graphics adapter (CGA). A graphics display adapter for MS-DOS computers that can display four colors simultaneously in a graphics mode.

Communication software. *See* Telecommunication software.

Compact disc. A 4.72-inch-wide plastic platter that stores digital data or music, encoded and read by laser (light) beam.

Compact disc audio (CD-Audio). A popular format for high-fidelity digital music. Each compact disc can store 74 minutes of sound with no degradation of quality during playback.

Compact disc interactive (CD-i). A system specification for an interactive audio, video, and computer system based on compact disc as the storage medium. CD-i uses an integrated player and is focused at the consumer and training markets.

Compact Disc-Read Only Memory (CD-ROM). A prerecorded, non-erasable disc that stores over 650MB of digital data.

Compact disc recordable (CD-R). A CD-ROM drive capable of recording compact discs in a format that is compatible with CD-ROM standards.

Composite video. A video signal that combines the colors and synchronization into one signal so it only requires one cable. Most televisions, videotape players, and videodisc players use composite video.

Compression. Technique used to reduce the amount of space needed to store video, images, sound, and so on.

Computer-based training. Training that is delivered through the medium of the computer. It is usually interactive and individualized in design.

Constant angular velocity (CAV). A videodisc format that allows the user to address each frame separately. Videodiscs recorded in the CAV format can store a maximum of 30 minutes of motion on each side of the videodisc.

Constant linear velocity (CLV). A videodisc format that can store 60 minutes of motion video on each side. Videodiscs recorded in the CLV format can play motion sequences, but they cannot display an individual frame.

Continuous voice recognition system. A voice recognition system that can translate phrases, rather than simply individual words.

Cross-platform. A software program that can run in both the Macintosh and MS-DOS environments.

Cycle time. The amount of time it takes a continuous simulation, such as a flight simulation, to make one complete loop through all calculations.

D

Daisychain. Connecting several CD-ROM players or other peripherals to the same computer port. Up to seven devices can be hooked up—one after another.

Data buffer. A temporary storage space on a CD-ROM drive. Many CD-ROMs provide a small data buffer (about 64K) to provide faster transfer to information.

Data bits. The number of bits that are used to define one character of information during telecommunications. Most BBS systems use eight data bits to define each character.

Data input gloves. Gloves worn in virtual reality applications that contain sensors and connections to provide the computer with information about the position and actions of the user's hands.

Data transfer rate. The number of kilobytes of information that can be transferred each second from the CD-ROM disc or other peripheral to the host computer. A single-speed CD-ROM drive has a data transfer rate of 150 K/sec; a quad-speed drive has 600 K/sec.

DataGlove. One brand of data input glove.

Dedicated telephone line. A normal telephone line that is used for nothing but telecommunications. This reduces the likelihood that someone will pick up an extension or otherwise interrupt while the modem is online.

Digital recording. A method of recording in which samples of the original analog signal are encoded as bits and bytes.

Digital Video Interactive (DVI). A technology for compressing and decompressing video and audio to create multimedia applications. DVI can store over an hour of full motion video on a compact disc.

Digital video. Video that is stored in bits and bytes on a computer. It can be manipulated and displayed on a computer screen.

Digitizing. The process of converting an analog signal into a digital signal.

Disc. Usually refers to a videodisc or compact disc. Computer diskettes are generally referred to as disks (with a "k") and videodiscs and other optical storage media are referred to as discs (with a "c").

Discrete voice recognition system. A voice recognition system that recognizes individual words and requires the speaker to pause after every word.

Disk cache. A software program that uses RAM to store data in order to speed up an application. Disk cache software is often used with CD-ROMs to improve the performance.

Double-speed drive. A CD-ROM drive that transfers data at 300 Kbytes/sec.—twice as fast as the original CD-Audio discs.

Downlink. A location that receives a video teleconference from a satellite.

DSP (Digital Signal Processor). A separate processor that is built into some of the digital audio cards. DSP processors help relieve the computer's CPU from processing all of the audio data.

DVI. *See* Digital Video Interactive.

E

Electronic mail (e-mail). Mail or communications that are sent and received through electronic, nonpaper methods.

Embedded training. Training that is integrated into an application program. A worker can call up the training as needed without exiting the application.

Ethernet. A baseband LAN communications standard developed by Xerox. Data transmission speed is typically 10 megabits per second.

Expert systems. An application of artificial intelligence that uses a knowledge base of human expertise to solve problems.

External calls. Some programs, such as authoring systems or expert system shells allow separate programs to be activated for complex calculations.

For example, an authoring system might not be able to display advanced digitized video, but it might have the capability to activate a separate program that can.

F

Facilitator. A person who is trained to help a group focus upon and solve a problem. Advanced software such as Group Decision Support Software often requires one participant to be a facilitator.

Facsimile machine (fax). An electronic device that transmits written or graphic material over telephone lines to other locations.

FDDI. *See* Fiber Distributed Digital Interface.

Feedback. Information that returns to the user of a system that reflects the impact of user interactions upon the system.

Fiber Distributed Digital Interface (FDDI). A data distribution standard that applies to LANs that use fiber optic cables.

Fiber optic cable. A cable that contains a fine strand of glass-like material. Light, not electricity, is conducted through the cable.

Field. One-half of a complete video scanning cycle (one-sixtieth of a second). Two fields make up a complete videodisc frame.

Field test. A preliminary trial prior to full implementation. Often used with newly developed training materials to uncover any remaining flaws.

File server. The computer in a LAN that stores and distributes the files for the workstations.

Flow chart. A graphic illustration that breaks a process into its individual components.

FM (frequency modulation). A technology used on digital audio cards to synthesize musical instruments with computerized tones.

Fractal compression. A technique that uses mathematics to analyze similarities in images and create algorithms for compression. Results in extremely large compression ratios.

Frame rate. The number of video frames displayed each second. The NTSC standard specifies 30 frames per second for full-motion video.

Frame number or address. Each frame on a videodisc has a unique number between 1 and 54,000. These numbers can be used to access the frame with the remote control, barcode reader, or computer.

Frame. A single, complete picture in a video recording; frames consist of two video fields.

Frame grabber. A device that converts a single analog video frame into digital format to store on a hard drive.

Freeze frame. Displaying a single frame that was originally produced as a part of a motion sequence.

Full-motion video. Video frames displayed at 30 frames per second.

G

Gateway. A computer in a LAN that links two dissimilar LANs. It is capable of translating data between the two LANs.

GDSS. *See* Group decision support system.

Graphical user interface (GUI). The technique of using a mouse and icons to select computer functions that was first widely used on the Apple Macintosh computers.

Graphics tablet. A computer device that converts hand-drawn images into digital information that can be displayed on computer screens.

Green book. The format standard for CD-i discs.

Group decisionware. Another name for Group Decision Support System software.

Group decision support system. A software program that is designed to help groups of people reach decisions on issues. It combines word processing, outlining, real time charting of voting, and a number of other functions.

Group consensus software. Another name for Group Decision Support System software.

Groupware. A generic term that is used to describe software and hardware such as electronic mail systems and desktop teleconferencing systems that are designed to be used by more than one person.

GUI. *See* Graphical user interface.

H

Handshake. Modem settings that must be matched before two computers can communicate through the modems.

Headset. Equipment that is worn on the head of a person working with a virtual reality application. Contains video display(s), audio system(s), and sensory equipment that provides the computer with information about the head motions of the user.

Hertz (Hz). Unit of measurement of frequency; numerically equal to cycles per second.

HFS (Hierarchical File System). The Apple HFS standard is used to create Macintosh-only CD-ROM discs; this standard is the same file format used on all Macintosh floppy disks and hard disks.

High Sierra. A format for CD-ROM data. This format is also known as ISO 9660 and it can be used for Macintosh or MS-DOS discs.

Host computer. The computer one calls when initiating telecommunications. It might be a mainframe, a LAN, or just another personal computer.

Hypermedia program. A software program that provides seamless access to text, graphics, audio, and video.

I

Icon. A graphic symbol that represents a program function. For example, a drawing of a pencil eraser might represent the "erase" function.

Image Capture. The process of digitizing a picture. While this term can be used with all image digitizing processes, it is most often used in reference to video digitizing of single images.

Inclusion. One of the characteristics of virtual reality. The user becomes a part of and contained within the virtual environment.

Indeo. A codec created by Intel to compress and decompress video.

Instructional Television Fixed Service (ITFS). A set of microwave frequencies that have been designated for use by educational facilities. Allows television transmissions over ranges of about 20 miles.

Integrated Services Digital Network (ISDN). A new technology for telephone systems that is totally digital. Computer data can be intermixed with voice communications.

Intelligent tutoring systems (ITS). An advanced form of computer-based training that utilizes artificial intelligence to custom fit the instruction to the individual.

Interactive video. A video presentation that interacts with the learner. Often uses videodisc technology, but digitized video is becoming more common.

Interactive videodisc (IVD). Generally refers to Level III interactivity, in which a computer is used to control a videodisc player.

Interfield flicker. The jitter that occurs on a video frame when the two fields do not match perfectly. Interfield flicker usually occurs when there is a large, rapid movement between the fields that constitute a single frame.

Internet. A network of networks connecting governmental institutions, military branches, educational institutions, and commercial companies.

ISDN. *See* Integrated Services Digital Network.

ISO 9660. A format for CD-ROM data that was established by the International Standards Organization. This format approximate the MS-DOS style of naming files, and it can be used for Macintosh or MS-DOS discs. Also known as High Sierra.

ITFS. *See* Instructional Television Fixed Service.

ITS. *See* Intelligent tutoring systems.

IVD. *See* interactive videodisc.

J

Jewel box. The little plastic boxes that compact discs come packaged in. These cannot be used as caddies to play the discs.

Job aid. A training device that is used on-the-job. It is often a simple outline of steps that were taught in greater detail at an earlier time.

Joint Photographic Expert Group (JPEG). An organization that has developed an international standard for compression and decompression of still images.

Joystick. An input device that can be used in place of a mouse or touch screen. The joystick resembles the control device in airplanes, so it is often used in airplane simulators.

JPEG. *See* Joint Photographic Expert Group.

Jukebox. CD-ROM drives that can hold several discs and switch between them to play the one that is requested by the computer.

Just in time (JIT). A parts delivery logistic process that has become popular in factory settings. When applied to training, it means delivering only the precise training that is needed at the time it is needed.

K

Keyword search. A search that allows the user to search the contents of all the electronic documents for a specific keyword or phrase. It usually provides a listing of the articles that contain the keyword and the number of hits (occurrences) of the keyword in each article.

Kilohertz (kHz). Unit of measurement of frequency; equal to 1,000 hertz.

L

Lag time. Related to cycle time. The delay in a simulation or virtual reality application between the input of information (for example, moving a flight control), and the displayed impact of that input. If lag time is unnaturally long due to slow calculations, the user can become disoriented.

LAN. *See* Local area network.

Laservision. An industry standard format for videodiscs. All consumer videodisc players are laservision compatible.

Learner interaction. The ability of a learner to provide input into an instructional program. Many programs are designed to interpret this input and modify the instruction based upon it.

Level I interactivity. Interactivity achieved when the videodisc player is controlled through the player, a remote control, or a barcode reader. The player is not connected to a computer.

Level II interactivity. Interactivity achieved when the videodisc contains a computer control program as well as the video material. The player is not connected to a computer.

Level III interactivity. Interactivity achieved when a computer is used to control the videodisc player.

Linear presentations. A presentation, such as a traditional slide show or videotape, that proceeds from beginning to end without changing direction.

Local area network (LAN). A system of interconnected computers. Usually located within one building or a set of adjacent buildings.

LocalTalk. A network standard used by Apple Macintosh computers. Uses shielded or unshielded twisted-pair wire.

Logoff. A simple command used in telecommunications to tell the host computer that the user is finished. Usually it is a choice from an on-screen menu, but sometimes the user actually types logoff or logout.

Logon. The procedure followed to start a telecommunication session. Often it requires the user to enter a name and a correct password.

Lossless compression. Compression programs that retain all of the information in the original file.

Lossy compression. Compression programs that discard some information during the reduction process.

Magneto-optical discs. Computer drives that allow you to write, erase, and rewrite on a compact disc. These drives use a combination of the technique used to save information on a hard drive (magnetic) and the technique used to store information on a CD-ROM (optical).

Manipulation. A characteristic of virtual reality applications. A user of a VR program can manipulate items within the environment, much as people can manipulate items within the real world.

Mean Time Between Failures (MTBF). An estimate (in hours) of how long a device, such as a hard drive, will last before requiring maintenance.

Megabit. One million bits.

Microsoft Extensions (MSCDEX). A software program by Microsoft Corporation that allows MS-DOS computers to communicate with a CD-ROM drive just like any other computer drive.

Microwave. A high-frequency transmission that can be used for television signals or computer data. Microwave transmissions are said to be line of sight, which means that they cannot pass through tall buildings or mountains.

MIDI (Musical Instrument Digital Interface). A standard for communicating musical information among computers and musical devices.

Mixed mode CD-ROM. Compact discs that contain both computer data and CD-Audio tracks. The computer data is generally recorded on the inner tracks of the disc, and the audio is recorded on the outer tracks.

Modem (MOdulator-DEModulator). Modems are used to link computers together through telephone lines. Modulation is the process of changing computer data into tones that can be sent through a telephone line, and demodulation is the process of changing the tones back into computer data.

Monitor. A visual display device capable of accepting both video and audio signals.

Moving Picture Coding Expert Group (MPEG). Working parties for standardization of motion video compression. MPEG-1 is used for linear video movies on compact discs; MPEG-2 is designed for broadcast digital video, and MPEG-3 is being developed for High Definition TV.

MPC. *See* Multimedia Personal Computer.

MPEG. *See* Moving Picture Coding Expert Group.

Multimedia Personal Computer (MPC). A standard that specifies hardware and software requirements for multimedia personal computers in the MS-DOS environment. The standard includes memory requirements, CD-ROM performance, display adapter, operating system, etc.

Multimedia. More than one medium. When applied to computer technology, it means some combination of alphanumerics, sound, still images, or motion images all delivered under the control of the computer.

Multi-session player. A CD-ROM player that can read discs that were recorded at several different times. For example, Photo-CD discs are often recorded in several sessions.

N

National Television Standards Committee (NTSC). This committee formulated the United States standard of 525 horizontal scan lines per frame at 30 frames per second for motion video and television.

Navigation. A characteristic of virtual reality applications. A person working with a VR program is able to move about throughout the virtual environment.

Network interface card (NIC). The interface card that is added to a computer to make it a LAN workstation. It determines the LAN standard for the network cable. Common standards are Arcnet, Ethernet, and Token-Ring.

NTSC. *See* National Television Standards Committee.

O

Online. Having a computer connected via modem and telephone lines to another computer.

Optical disc. A disc that is encoded and read with a beam of light. Usually refers to a compact disc or videodisc.

Optical character recognition (OCR). Software designed to convert text on paper into digital form. Many scanners provide OCR software.

Orange book. The format standard for WORM (Write Once-Read Many) compact discs.

Overlay. Placing one image over another. Normally, parts of both images are visible. For example, with the right equipment, video from a disc player can be overlayed onto an instructional screen on a computer monitor.

P

Packet switching. A transmission technique commonly used in LANs. Packets are transmitted in an intermixed manner, with each one going to its predetermined destination. This allows all workstations on a LAN equal access to files.

Packet. A grouping of binary digits, often a portion of a larger file. Treated within a LAN as an entity.

PAL (Phased Alternate Line). PAL is the video/television standard used in Europe, Australia, and other countries. It specifies 625 horizontal scan lines at 25 frames per second.

Parity. A specific structure added to the data bits that are going into a modem to check for errors when the data bits arrive at the destination. Parity is usually defined as even, odd, or none. None means that no parity error checking is conducted.

Performance support system (PSS). An integrated set of computer programs that provide workers with the information or training they need, when they need it.

Photo-CD (photographic compact disc). A compact disc format developed by the Kodak company to store photographic images on a compact disc.

Picture stops. A frame on a videodisc where the player will automatically stop and wait for the user to press play.

Pixel. A single dot or point of an image on a computer screen. Pixel is a contraction of the words picture element.

PLV (production level video). A DVI format that provides more than one hour of full-screen/full-motion video on a compact disc. The PLV format requires that the files be sent to a mainframe for compression.

Power Glove. A brand of data input glove.

Printer server. A computer on a LAN that runs software to control one or more shared printers.

Proprietary controller interface. A computer interface that is designed to operate with a specific peripheral, such as a specific CD-ROM player.

Protocol. In telecommunications, refers to the complete structure of the information that is going from one computer to the other.

Proximity search. A search that specifies the closeness of the keywords within the document. For example, the user can specify that the keywords must be in the same paragraph or be less than five words apart.

PSS. *See* Performance support system.

Quad-speed CD-ROM drive. A CD-ROM drive that has a data transfer rate four times faster (600 Kbytes/sec) than the original compact discs (150 Kbytes/sec).

QuickTime. A file format that allows Macintosh computers to compress and play digitized video movies with software compression.

R

Receiver. A visual display device capable of receiving and displaying a broadcast signal.

Red book. The format used to record music on a CD-Audio disc.

Redundant Arrays of Inexpensive Disks (RAID). Process of using two or more hard drives working together in a file server to provide levels of error recovery and fault tolerance.

Resolution. The sharpness or clarity of a computer screen. Monitors with more lines and pixels of information have better resolution.

Rewritable compact discs. Computer drives that allow you to write, erase, and rewrite on a compact disc.

RGB (Red Green Blue). The three primary colors used for the computer video signal.

Ring network. A LAN topology in which data are transmitted in one circular direction among workstations.

RS-232. An interface frequently used for transmitting data between computers or from a peripheral (such as a videodisc player) to a computer.

RTV (real time video). A DVI format that can be produced on a microcomputer. RTV generally results in digital video that displays in one-quarter of the screen.

Runtime. A reduced version of a development program, such as an authoring system, that allows a lesson to be delivered to a learner, but not modified by the learner.

S

Sampling rate. The number of intervals per second that a digital value is stored for a sound waveform. The sampling rate affects sound quality; the higher the sampling rate, the better the sound quality.

Scan. A mode of play in which the player skips over several frames at a time. Scanning can be done in forward or reverse.

Scripting language. A set of verbal commands that are included in some icon and menu-based development systems. The scripting language allows complex computer instructions to be created.

SCSI (Small Computer Serial Interface). An interface controller that allows several peripherals to be connected to the same port on a computer.

SCSI-2. An improved, updated form of SCSI.

SECAM (sequential color with memory). The color video/television standard used in France. It is similar to, but incompatible with, NTSC and PAL.

Sequencer. A device that records MIDI events and data.

Simulation. The set of rules or algorithms that define a particular object or event.

Simulator. A device that runs a simulation. Often driven by a computer.

Single-session player. A CD-ROM player that can only read discs that were recorded in one session. If a multi-session disc is played in this player, it will only read the part of the disc that was recorded first.

Single-speed CD-ROM drive. A CD-ROM drive with a data transfer rate of 150 Kbytes/sec.

Slide table. A feature of some presentation software that allows a person to view and arrange a number of reduced images.

Snapshot. *See* Image Capture.

Sound module. A peripheral for MIDI that uses an electronic synthesizer to generate the sounds of musical instruments.

Star network. A LAN topology in which all workstations are connected directly to a central location, often the file server.

Start bits. Every character of information that goes through a modem is preceded with one or more start bits. Most common modem protocols use one start bit.

Step frame. A function of a videodisc player that moves from one frame to the next (can be forward or reverse).

Still frame. A single videodisc frame that is presented as a static image (not a part of a moving sequence).

Stop bits. Every character of information that goes through a modem ends with one or more stop bits. Most common BBS systems use one stop bit.

S-Video. A video signal that has a higher quality than composite video. Brightness and color are divided into two separate channels. (Also called Y/C).

Synthesizer. A musical instrument or device that generates sound electronically.

System operator (sysop). The person in charge of maintaining a BBS or LAN. The sysop monitors the system, answers questions, and checks files that are up-loaded.

T

T1 line. A special type of leased telephone line that transmits digital information at a high rate. These lines are much more expensive than regular telephone lines.

T3 line. A special type of leased telephone line that transmits digital information at even higher rates than T1 lines.

Telecommunication software. Program used to allow the computer to communicate through a modem. Most software of this type dials the requested number and sets the modem for the system that is being called.

Teleconferencing. Electronic techniques that are used to allow several people at two or more locations to communicate.

Templates. Predefined colors, text fonts, and patterns that can be selected for use. Common in authoring systems and presentation systems.

Terminal emulation. Most mainframe computers are designed to communicate with specific workstations called terminals. For a microcomputer to communicate with a mainframe, the microcomputer telecommunication software must be able to perform like, or emulate, an appropriate terminal. Most telecommunication software can emulate a variety of common computer terminals.

Terrain model. The information in a simulation that tells the computer how to construct the visible terrain while the simulation runs.

Text-to-speech synthesis. Sounds created by applying computer algorithms to text to produce spoken words.

Thinnet. A type of coaxial cable that is used in local area networks. As its name implies, it is thinner than standard coaxial cable.

Timeline. A method of creating a presentation program based upon accurate timing. Popular for music and motion video applications.

Token Ring. A network standard that uses a ring topology with token-passing techniques to prevent data collisions. Transmission rates are 4 or 16 megabits per second, depending upon interface cards and type of cable.

Token. A special message or flag used in some LANs. The token is passed from workstation to workstation, and the workstation that has the token can transmit. This prevents data collisions.

Tracking. The electronics and sensors in virtual reality systems that allow the computer to follow the motions of the user.

Transition. Visual effects, such as dissolves or wipes, that take place as a program moves from one image or screen of information to the next.

Tree topology. A LAN topology in which all workstations are connected to a branching central transmission cable.

Triple-speed CD-ROM drive. A drive that transfers data at 450 Kbytes/sec.—three times as fast as the original CD-Audio discs.

Truncation. A search technique used in accessing electronic databases that allows for alternate endings to key words.

Twisted-pair cable. Two wires twisted together. This type of cable is often used for telephone communications.

U

Uplink. The site for a video conference from which a signal is sent up to a satellite.

Upload. The process of sending a complete file to the host computer.

V

VGA. *See* Video graphics array.

Video graphics array (VGA). A graphics display adapter for MS-DOS computers that can display up to 16 colors simultaneously with a resolution of 640 x 480 pixels.

Video conferencing. Transmitting motion video and audio to two or more locations for the purpose of interactive conferencing.

Video for Windows (VFW). A file format that allows MS-DOS computers to compress and play digitized video movies with software compression.

Video-CD. Compact discs that are designed to delivery full-motion video. These discs can store up to 74 minutes of video; however, they require special video decoder hardware and/or software.

Video-in-a-window. A technique which passes analog video through an interface card and displays it on a computer screen in real time.

Virtual reality. An approximation of reality. Advanced three-dimensional simulations are often used to create virtual reality environments.

Visual database. A videodisc that consists of primarily individual pictures. It is designed to be displayed as still frames rather than played as motion.

VR. *See* Virtual reality.

W

WAN. *See* Wide area network.

Waveform. The shape of a sound depicted graphically as amplitude over time.

Wavetable synthesis. Wavetables store prerecorded samples of actual sounds and musical instruments on digital audio boards for MIDI play back.

Wide area network (WAN). One or more LANs that are interconnected, but distributed over a large area. Usually some form of leased communication line is used for the long distance connections.

Wildcards. A search technique used to access electronic documents or databases that allows alternate spellings within words. For example, a wildcard (*) can be used to search for WOM*N, yielding either WOMAN or WOMEN.

Within-frame compression. Discards redundant information on each screen. Also known as intraframe or spatial compression.

Workstation. Individual microcomputer on a LAN that is used by employees and managers to run programs.

WORM (Write Once-Read Many). Refers to a technology that can record (but not erase) a compact disc. WORM discs are not compatible with most CD-ROM drives; therefore, they are less popular than the CD-R discs.

Y

Yellow book. A format standard used for CD-ROM discs.

INDEX

B

C

N

O

P

Q

R

V

W

Y

Z